Touching the Father's Heart through Prayer

LISA PERNA

Please note that the author has chosen to capitalize certain pronouns in Scripture (He, Him, and His) that refer to the Father, Son, and Holy Spirit. This may differ from some publishers' styles. Take note that the name satan and related names are not capitalized. She chooses not to acknowledge him, even to the point of violating accepted grammatical rules.

Some names have been changed to protect the privacy of these individuals. Other people have given their permission to use their names and testimony.

One story includes some graphic content. However, the author wanted to stay true to the vision as the Lord showed it to her, so she have left the wording as is.

Print ISBN: 979-8-218-12240-9

This book is dedicated to
Papa God, my heavenly Father;
Jesus; and the Holy Spirit
for being my constant love and support.

My father, William Palieri, who loved the Lord, rejoiced in my calling.
He was my biggest cheerleader on earth and is now cheering me on in
heaven.

My children, Alexander and Samantha Perna, are two of the greatest gifts
God has ever given me.

Acknowledgments

It takes a village to raise a child and a tribe to birth a book. I cannot begin to thank all of the people for the support and encouragement I have received over the years to write a book and share my stories. Your prayers, love and pushing have birthed this!

Special thanks to the following:

First, thank you to my husband, Ron, I mean Rob, for being the man behind the woman. You have allowed me to follow the Lord even when the cost was high. The support at my conferences, broadcasts, and even in writing this book that you thought should take three months has been your greatest display of love to me.

To my mom, Stephanie Palieri, and my siblings, Rik Palieri, Marianna Holzer, Tina Riegel, and David Palieri. My nieces and nephews, cousins Laurie Raspantini and her children, Cheryl Ferguson, Christina Miller, Peter Miller, and the Perna family. We all have stories to share. Thank you for being a part of mine. Thank you for all the encouragement you have given me throughout my life and for giving me material for this book.

Thank you to my spiritual mommas and poppas: Karen Arias, Robin and Roger Fields, Margie Moormann, Apostle Michael Fram, Pastor Gary Fishman, and Russ Painter. I don't know where I would be without your prayers, wisdom, support, and love. You all have journeyed with me not only through this book but helped to navigate me back to my purpose. I love you all so very much.

Thank you to my Daddy's Girls: Lila Shaw, Amie Roger, Debbie Kitterman, Toni Imsen, Ginny Wilcox, Kelly McCann, Dericklyn Parker, Melody Paasch, Shelly Vargo, Sheila Bruce, Judy Jones, Julie Jewell, Ryan and Kelly Faulker. Thank you for all the love, encouragement, support, friendship, and guidance that you have provided me with over the years. You have all been a safe place for me. I love you more than words can ever express.

Thank you to my GGs and BGs: [LT1] Ryan and Mary Busey, Rebecca Burnett, Amy Graff, Michelle Shelly Warriner, Grandma Linda Sheals, Audrey DeMola, Robin Segnitz, Stephanie Anderson, Linda Jones, Tara Howanice, Kim Schultz, Jana Jones, Paige Robinson, Rebecca Kirby, Theresa Bianco, Liz Lemgruber, and James Sheals. Your prayers have availed much! You have been my answer to prayer. I cannot thank you enough for what you have done. You guys were the game changer in my life and ministry.

Cathy Franz and the Hozdovic clan: You have supported me and loved me through thick and thin. I am eternally thankful for having a safe place to share my crazy God stories. I love you for opening up your home, heart, and life to me and my family.

Thank you to all my spiritual children especially Kara Birkey, Brittney Anderson, Carrie Price-Knospe, and Gloria and Chris Pourciaux you guys have cheered me on, prayed for me and spoke the heart of God into my life!

How do I thank the man that brought the scriptures alive and gave it a voice that spoke to my heart? Not only has Dr. Brian Simmons changed how I read the scriptures, but how I interact with the Father. I cannot thank you enough for writing the Passion Translation version of the bible. I am beyond humbled that you would honor me and write the forward to this book. You and Candice are special gifts that Papa has blessed me with and I am so very grateful.

Thank you for those who have read endorsed my book your words have blessed me beyond words Jeremy Mangerchine, Jesse Birkey, Tom Loud, Nick Padovani, Randy Kay, Robert Hotchkin, Julie Lavender, Steve Rizzo and Shaun Tabatt.

Thank you to those who have been so gracious and allowed me to share your stories Dana Keating, Tatayana Poletayeva, Kayman and Liz Culley, and Anthony Turner.

Thank you to those friends who stayed with me on this crazy God adventure, Rosanna Dietrich, Magdalena Rosiak, Lisa Ciullo, Mary Semplenski, Tracey and Bobby Noesner, Tyler Johnson, Kathy Satch, Joni McKenna, Tracy Mihalak, Paul Wilcox, Todd and Tamara Engwall. Hanging out with you and Jesus has been the best!

Special thank you to all those who have supported my ministry; Anya Martyanova, Uncle Larry Norris, Max Probasco, Joe and Laraine Conte, Ron and Renee Joelson, Yesenia and Jose Bonilla, Juanita and Jack Miller, Margie Fleurant, John and Nancy Natale, Alizanette and Burt Rodriguez, Sandra Russo, Lynda and Hank Marsman, Toni Bogart-Syvrud, Andrea Joy Moede, Maggie Judd, Joanne Poppas, Lori and Jim La Maire, and Steve Hampton. Your friendship, constant encouragement, and prayers have blessed me beyond words.

Special thank you to Lorri Dresbach for my beautiful cover and my editor Lisa Thompson. You ladies have helped give birth to this book. I will forever be grateful for all you did to make my dream a reality. Thank you to Steve Bremner for putting it all together!

Thank you to all my listeners and those who have sown into my life. May Papa bless you abundantly!

Endorsements

Compelled to read Lisa Perna's revelatory book, *Touching the Father's Heart through Prayer*, for the second time, I realized that her stories, wisdom, and heavenly impartations were increasing my prayer life to affect a greater outpouring of God's fullness. That is saying a lot for someone who has died and seen Jesus face-to-face, because I thought that my encounter in heaven had maximized my prayer life, given that my faith had been validated through my afterlife experience. But Lisa's keen ability to elucidate the power of prayer through story teaches fundamental truths that can only be gleaned through the author's deep relationship with our Creator.

I so appreciate that Lisa points out in her book that "God is a God of restoration, and He always finds a way to give back what is taken away." Until we can grasp this truth with all our hearts, we will continue to struggle in life. That the author provides such practical teachings to live fully in the Spirit can only be explained by Lisa's own character and love for God. Lisa exudes the character of Jesus—I know that full well. I cannot speak more highly of a person than to make that statement. I trust that you, like me, will be made spiritually richer through reading this profound book. Thank you, Lisa, for gifting us with this treasure trove of life-changing words.

— RANDY KAY BEST-SELLING AUTHOR,
REVELATIONS FROM HEAVEN AND *DYING TO MEET JESUS*, FORMER CORPORATE CEO AND FOUNDER OF RANDY KAY MINISTRIES

For many Christians, prayer is one of the most frustrating aspects of our faith journey. We wonder if our words make it past the ceiling, let alone are heard in heaven. If you've wrestled with this too, that's precisely why you need this book.

Through relatable and practical examples, Lisa shows readers how to develop a deep and intimate friendship with God that will unlock the world-altering and destiny-shifting prayers you've always longed to pray.

— SHAUN TABATT, PUBLISHING EXECUTIVE,
DESTINY IMAGE

As I read *Touching the Father's Heart through Prayer*, Song of Songs 4:16 pressed itself against my heart. "May your awakening breath blow upon my life until I am fully yours."

This book is a testimony to that desperate, beautiful plea as it worked through Lisa's heart and onto the pages ahead. Not only will the stories and insightful teaching she shares touch and encourage you, but they'll inspire you to live a life wholly devoted to God. To experience Him. To find new ways to love Him. To be loved by Him.

I'm blessed to know Lisa and honored to experience the expressions of her heart contained in this book.

— JESSE BIRKEY AUTHOR *FINDING HOME,*
MARRIAGE WHAT'S THE POINT?, LIFE RESURRECTED,
AND COME ALIVE WITH JESUS

Touching the Father's Heart through Prayer is an inspiring and engaging read. Lisa Perna beautifully shares her own experiences and invites you along for the journey. She lays a solid biblical foundation for the importance of prayer and relationship with the Father. Lisa also models what it looks like to have big faith and holy boldness, to walk in obedience, and to believe in God for the impossible.

In *Touching the Father's Heart through Prayer,* Lisa shows the endless possibilities and adventures that await each one of us when we choose to pursue a loving relationship with the Father, Son, and Holy Spirit.

— DEBBIE KITTERMAN, FOUNDER, DARE2HEAR
MINISTRIES; FOUNDER, SOUND THE CALL, LLC.;
INTERNATIONAL SPEAKER; PODCASTER; PASTOR;
BLOGGER AT DARE2HEAR.COM; DARE2HEAR THE
PODCAST; D2HTRAINING.COM, AUTHOR *LEGACY:*
THE LOST ART OF BLESSING, THE GIFT OF PROPHETIC
ENCOURAGEMENT: HEARING THE WORDS OF GOD
FOR OTHERS, THE GIFT OF PROPHETIC
ENCOURAGEMENT BIBLE STUDY: LIVING A LIFESTYLE
OF ENCOURAGEMENT, AND RELEASING GOD'S HEART
THROUGH HEARING HIS VOICE.

Whether you are hungry for fresh Bible teaching, thirsty for testimonies to inspire your own supernatural adventures, or just need to take first steps, Lisa Perna's book, *Touching the Father's Heart through Prayer*, will open up a whole new realm of possibilities that will blow your prayer life open wide.

Fresh Bible teaching, thrilling testimonies, and practical first-step prayers—you will encounter all this and more in Lisa Perna's powerful new book.

This book opens up new realms and possibilities that will blow your mind and inspire your own supernatural prayer adventures.

— JULIE LAVENDER BROADCASTER, AUTHOR,
SPEAKER, MUSICIAN

Have you heard that learning to pray comes from praying? As Lisa's spiritual momma, I have witnessed her growth into an amazing, mature prayer warrior, intercessor, and exhorter of the Word of God and lover of Jesus.

This compelling book will bring you into her prayer experiences of praying in trust and with full confidence in God's love so that you have a deep understanding of the extensive ways we can communicate in prayer with our Papa God.

— MARGIE MOORMANN "MOMMA MARGIE"
INTERNATIONAL SPEAKER, PASTOR, MENTOR, AND
AUTHOR OF *ANGELS SING, BUT DO THEY DANCE?"*
PAPA GOD'S HIDEAWAY MINISTRIES

Touching the Father's Heart through Prayer is not a mechanical textbook on prayer but rather flows from Lisa's pure passion to touch the heart of the Father. She desires that every reader would experience the joy, power, and breakthrough that transpires when prayer becomes a back-and-forth flow as a river that connects heaven and earth. This book will revolutionize your prayer life and launch you into a place of greater intimacy and spirit-to-spirit encounters with your heavenly Father.

We are living in a world that is moving at an incredible pace. We can easily get lost in false truths and misplaced feelings.

We all need something that can place us at the helm and guide us to steer the course of our lives, especially when the storms of misfortune are falling upon us. That something is God.

Lisa Perna has created a wonderful book of truth and heartfelt stories that will show you how to connect and communicate with the almighty power within. If you're seeking a better way to live or if your life isn't working on any level, then *Touching the Father's Heart through Prayer* is a must-read.

Lisa has given us an absolutely precious gift with this book. The Lord has given her the uncommon ability to lead the reader through deep and intimate waters with an easy and fun-to-read book. Read this book with expectancy in your heart. Anticipate your Father touching your own heart and speaking right within your spirit as you follow her on this journey. Thank you, Lisa, for sharing your story.

— NICK PADOVANI PASTOR OF THE ALMOND BRANCH, AUTHOR OF *THE SONG OF THE AGES*

Lisa Perna is a very special person, and the Lord has used her to reach many people with His words of wisdom, comfort, and encouragement. In her book, *Touching the Father's Heart through Prayer*, the reader is drawn into a journey that broadens and deepens with each chapter, a journey into deeper intimacy and awareness of the Lord. This book is written in a style that makes the reader feel as if Lisa is a personal friend sitting across from you at a table and personally sharing her great testimony and experiences with Jesus. This book shares foundational truths, and Lisa builds on them chapter upon chapter, bringing a follower of Jesus into a fully matured and balanced relationship with Him. Lisa moves powerfully in the prophetic and with great compassion, she has poured into the lives of many, including myself. Read this book, learn from Lisa's amazing adventures with the Lord, and start a life of experiencing the deeper, fuller, and richer things of God in a marvelous new way.

— PASTOR TOM LOUD AUTHOR OF *UNLOCKING KINGDOM POWER*

A commercial for US Navy on TV back in the early '80s coined the phrase: "It's not just a job, it's an adventure." I have often thought about that phrase through the years when I think of Lisa Perna. My relationship with her dates back to about 2016. She has always been wide-eyed and viewed her encounters and experiences with Abba as adventures.

This book is just that. She takes you, the reader, on a series of adventures that she has lived through, and through her journeys, her goal is to bring you into the same intimate relationship with Papa that she has developed.

I have always told her that she has a natural, supernatural way of disarming people and putting them at ease with her easy-going, story-telling way of communicating. What you hold in your hands is a fantastic example of exactly that. You will glean from the wisdom nuggets and principles in her stories and, yes, her adventures.

Let me encourage you to take a journey, and go on an adventure with Lisa through the pages of this book, *Touching the Father's Heart through Prayer.*

— APOSTLE MICHAEL FRAM PROPHETIC DESTINY
MINISTRIES INT'L, SAYREVILLE, NEW JERSEY;
AUTHOR, *FROM FATHER TO SON: AN EXAMPLE OF
MULTIGENERATIONAL SONSHIP*

Lisa is a mother to many, the kind of mother who lives from the heart of the Father. She sees deep into the essence of man, connects authentically, and passionately loves people toward freedom. This kind of love doesn't just happen. It is not manufactured or contrived. It comes from the profound revelation gleaned from consistent time spent with a good and loving God.

I wish you could know Lisa. I wish *everyone* could know Lisa. She's the real deal. Fortunately, she has written this book that is overflowing with inspirational encounters that will encourage and empower each of you to experience for yourself the richness of the heart of God.

Let her story and insights catapult you into your own adventure with God.

— JEREMY MANGERCHINE ARTIST, AUTHOR, *THE LONGEST BRIDGE ACROSS WATER, THE TABLE AND THE DREAM,* AND *THE QUITTERS MANUAL*

Everything God did for us through the gift of His Son speaks of His great desire—His hunger and willingness to do whatever it took—to be in relationship with you. But you do not have to wait to get to heaven to enjoy that fullness of relationship. You can enter it right here and right now. That's a big part of what prayer is all about. Lisa Perna's new book, *Touching the Father's Heart through Prayer,* will certainly help take the power and impact of your prayer life to a new level. But even more, it will help unlock new levels of intimacy, connection, and relationship with your heavenly Father. Lisa reveals how prayer can be more—*much* more—than simply a long list of requests. Read this book to discover how prayer can usher you into realms of deep-unto-deep, heart-to-heart union with your heavenly Father.

— ROBERT HOTCHKIN FOUNDER, ROBERT HOTCHKIN MINISTRIES/MEN ON THE FRONTLINES ROBERTHOTCHKIN.COM

Foreword

Every day, the God of love wants to meet with you. In the chamber room of His heart, a sacred place is reserved for you. It is where lovers meet. It is the place of longing, the place of passion, the place of prayer.

I hear an invitation from heaven. It is the Father calling out your name. He is asking you to arise and pray. If only you knew how sweet your voice is each time you call out to Him, it would bring you into the secret chamber of His heart over and over. Jesus calls to you: "How lovely you look there hidden in My love. Let Me hear your heart's cry, and I will answer you. Your voice is music to My ears—sweet, pleasing, and acceptable to Me." He's waiting and longing to commune with you.

My heart sings when I come before the Mighty One. Joy floods my soul as I call out to Him and know that He is waiting for me. What can be more exciting than coming before the God of Glory and spilling out our hearts to Him? It is intoxicating to the soul. Prayer is more than transactional, more than asking and receiving—it is communing, sharing life together, dropping our distractions at His feet, and basking in His burning presence. Prayer is entering the ecstasy of our union with Christ. Don't be surprised if something begins to burn inside your heart the next time you pray.

The Father's delight is to make us into a walking prayer-meeting. We carry the Christ within us and can literally pray without ceasing. Each day, each moment, we hear the invitation to pray. Prayer is very simple. We don't have to strive to touch God's heart. When we are in His presence, a simple and short prayer can be enough for us to express our adoration and worship to Him. There is something powerful about simple prayers that move God's heart:

- "I worship You, Father."
- "Let Your beloved Son kiss my heart."
- "I surrender my soul to you, my Father."
- "I love you, God."

When I am troubled, I step into heaven's peace through prayer. My quiet adoration silences my internal strife. While preaching on the mighty power of prayer, the famous British preacher Charles Spurgeon cried out: "The very act of prayer is a blessing. To pray is, as it were to bathe oneself in a cool stream, and so to escape from the heat of earth's summer sun. To pray is to mount on eagle's wings above the clouds and soar to heaven where God dwells."[1]

Reading through Lisa Perna's remarkable book, *Touching the Father's Heart through Prayer*, left me longing to step into that sacred chamber. Her life story is a testimony to the power of prayer. I know you are going to love this book! It will stir your soul to become a walking prayer-meeting. You have a sweet voice that fills the heavens when you pray. You—yes, you!—can touch the heart of Father God and fill Him with delight as you lay out the pieces of your life in prayer. God is ready to drench you with the Spirit of Prayer that will sustain you in the days ahead. I thank God that

Lisa has given us a path to power, a way to walk in intimacy with God. Get ready to see breakthroughs and miracles as you read this glorious message of *Touching the Father's Heart through Prayer*.

Dr. Brian Simmons
Passion & Fire Ministries

Introduction

What is prayer, and what is its purpose? Prayer is a conversation or the communication we have with God. It's a spiritual expression or a position we take when looking for supernatural guidance, assistance, or intervention from the spiritual realms of heaven. At its very core, prayer reminds us of the limitations we have as humans and the need for the unlimited power of God. Although we were created to be different, the one thing we all share is the ability to interact with our heavenly Father.

The level of engagement we have with a person all depends on the amount of time or the closeness we have with that individual. It's the same with God. In our relationship with Him, we learn His personality and the ways we touch His heart. In prayer, we are looking for Him to move on our requests as a good father provides for his children. God has no favorites, but He wants to have individual and personal relationships with all of us.

My prayer for you, the reader, is that you will see the importance of building a beautiful, loving, strong friendship with your heavenly

Father. Once you discover the power that lies in relationship with God, your prayers will move mountains.

CHAPTER 1
Words of God—Praying the Scripture

But if you live in life-union with me and if my words live powerfully
within you—then you can ask whatever you desire and it will be done.
~ John 15:7

I never in a million years thought that I would be writing a book, especially a book on prayer. I love to pray, and I've been praying ever since I was a child. For some reason, my prayers have moved heaven. The first answered prayer I ever saw was at the age of seven. My baby brother accidentally found my father's tranquilizers and swallowed a bunch of his pills. I prayed, asking God to save my little brother from dying. It was a simple prayer from a child, believing that the God of the universe would hear me and do as I had begged Him to do.

I didn't need to hear any testimony from a person or be convinced that God heals from someone speaking from a pulpit. Something inside me knew for certain He could do it. God answered many of my prayers, not because of my words or because I followed any protocol or specific formula. For some reason, I had favor with the

1

Lord, but a point came in my walk with God that I had to go deeper.

When I was a teenager and a newly born-again Christian, I got my first Bible. The Southern Baptist church I attended wanted me to memorize Scripture. According to them, I needed God's Word deeply engraved on my heart. I memorized and prayed only three verses, but they would be a life source in times of trouble. Those Scriptures that I memorized worked.

1. "But seek ye first the kingdom of God, and his righteousness; and all these things shall be added unto you" (Matthew 6:33 KJV).
2. "For God so loved the world that He gave His only begotten Son, that whoever believes in Him should not perish but have everlasting life" (John 3:16 NKJV).
3. "But He answered and said, 'It is written, Man shall not live by bread alone, but by every word that proceeds from the mouth of God'" (Matthew 4:4 NKJV).

I would pray these Scriptures when I needed God the most. If I were having a bad dream, my spirit knew that I could chase that demon away by using the Word of God. I would recite it over and over again in my dream until that dream would change. The funny part is, I didn't even realize then that Jesus used the same Scripture in Matthew 4:4 (originally found in Deuteronomy 8:3) when He was speaking with satan in the wilderness. If that verse worked for Jesus and for me, then why wouldn't it work for you too? The Word of God is a powerful weapon that calls forth a response from heaven.

Now God wanted me to know Him in a deeper way through the Bible and understand Him according to the Word. John 1:1 says, "In the beginning was the Word, and the word was with God and the Word was God" (NKJV). John was the first book of the Gospels I ever read and my introduction to the Word of God. Maybe I wanted to get to know God through His Word as much as He wanted me to get to know Him. As I read through each chapter, the verses almost came alive, and for the first time, it felt as if I could really understand it.

I came from a Catholic household, where the Bible was only read by the priest during mass. In my Saturday morning religious education class (CCD), we were given the following prayers. The first and most important one was the "Our Father," followed by "Hail, Mary" and the "Glory Be to Father." I didn't use the other two unless I was at church, but I prayed the "Our Father" prayer all the time. I didn't comprehend the perfection of this prayer until God helped me understand it. The disciples asked Jesus how they should pray, and He answered them by saying,

> In this manner, therefore, pray:
> Our Father in heaven,
> Hallowed be Your name.
> Your kingdom come.
> Your will be done
> On earth as it is in heaven.
> Give us this day our daily bread.
> And forgive us our debts,
> As we forgive our debtors.
> And do not lead us into temptation,
> But deliver us from the evil one.
> For Yours is the kingdom and the power and the glory
> forever. Amen. (Matthew 6:9–13 NKJV)

This perfect prayer starts by declaring who God really is, not just a superior being who has all power but a Father. He is a loving and good Father who cares deeply for all His children. Jesus is inviting us to be known as God's child. It goes on to say that our Father is holy and holiness is in His name. We ask for God's kingdom or His way of living to come and be established here on earth. This prayer also tells us that He will provide all we need, and all we need to do is simply ask. Jesus tells us to ask for forgiveness for all our sins because God forgives us. In addition, we need to forgive others for making mistakes. Lastly, we can pray for protection against the devil and be released from his control.

This prayer not only taught the disciples the way to pray but illustrates the way we can touch the heart of God so that our prayers are answered. First, we need to call Him Father; in the Old Testament, God calls Himself a Father to Israel. (See Isaiah 63:16.) In this Scripture, Jesus gave His disciples and us the permission to use the word *Father*. This personalization of God brings us into a relationship rather than into the slavery of religion. The rest of the prayer is our assurance of all that God will do for His children.

By using the Scriptures, we can know the promises of God and manifest these same promises in prayer. Jesus the Word came to show the disciples that those words spoken through the prophets didn't lie and that the Father is true to his word. Another way to use the Scripture is to war against the powers of darkness. The words we use are powerful weapons—we don't understand that even the angels harken or listen to the Word of God. The angels, even fallen ones, must obey His word. Everything we read in the Bible that Jesus spoke is powerful. When we hear these Scriptures, our spirit rises within us.

In Hebrews, the living Word of God is compared to the sword of the Spirit, and it is a mighty weapon used for the pulling down of strongholds. "For the word of God is alive and active. Sharper than any double-edged sword, it penetrates even to dividing soul and spirit, joints and marrow; it judges the thoughts and attitudes of the heart" (Hebrews 4:12). If the Word of God has now been weaponized as an instrument of war that was good enough for

Jesus to use in the wilderness, then the Word of God is powerful enough for you to use too. So the question remains, how do we effectively use the Word of God and make sure that it's touching the heart of God?

I have used the Word of God in prayer in a very unconventional way because I wasn't planning on using it. As I stated, as a Catholic, I really didn't know the Word of God. Once I started learning the Bible, the Holy Spirit began putting it in my heart so that I could recall it. I was now using the Word of God in my prayer time, even when I didn't think I knew it. Each time I began praying, the words would bubble up from my spirit. The Scriptures would pop into my head as if someone were reading them. God was showing me that He was in my time with Him and even though I didn't think the Word of God was powerful, He did.

The best example that I can give is when I used the Word of God while praying with my sister. I went to visit my family in Florida. My younger sister, Tina, was taking care of my mom and dad. My older brother, Rik, and his wife, Marianna, had come for a visit as well. It was a family reunion of sorts. I hadn't really spent much time with my siblings since I turned my life over to God. I felt this was an assignment from Him, and my sister would be my first priority.

We decided to take a drive out to my old stomping grounds and visit the beach. We were sitting in the car when she turned to me and asked, "Why are you so happy when I'm so sad?" I told her that I had dealt with a lot of my sadness with God and He had healed me. She asked, "If God could heal you, can He heal me as well?"

I said, "Of course, He can! Would you like me to pray for you?"

She looked at me and shrugged. "Sure, why not?" I began to pray for her and told her that I knew she had some unforgiveness that she needed to deal with. She looked me in the eye and shook her head. "No, I don't."

I knew in my heart that she really did. I said, "Tina, you have all this anger, and it's eating you up. It's time for you to be free, so let's get rid of this unforgiveness once and for all."

I started to pray, and she started to act weird. I told her, "Okay, I'm going to pray that God shows you your unforgiveness toward people. You're just going to start thinking of people that might've hurt you. The Holy Spirit will begin to bring those people to your memory, and as each person pops into your head, so simply say 'I forgive you.'"

She looked at me, her forehead scrunched up. "So God is going to show me who I have not forgiven?"

I replied, "Yes, and then you just forgive them."

She smirked and looked at me. "Really? It's that simple?"

"Yes. Forgiveness really *is* that simple. Once you forgive others and yourself, then you have closed the door so that the enemy can no longer steal your joy. When you forgive others, then God forgives you." I laid my hand on her head and began to pray in the spirit.

Slowly, people started to come to her mind. As she remembered each person, she said, "I forgive you." As we were going deeper into prayer, the Holy Spirit brought more and more people to her mind. Some of these memories surprised her. She thought that she hurt them and they probably had unforgiveness toward her. We were laughing and having a good time, quickly forgiving all these people from her past. Suddenly, the atmosphere in the car changed, and her face transformed so that she looked like a pig. My stomach sank as we had hit a very hard and tender place of extreme hurt.

I asked, "Who just popped into your head?" Her lips trembled as she blurted out the name of the perpetrator who had stolen so much of her life. This person would not be as simple to forgive as the others had been. Tears dripped down her face, and her breathing grew labored as if she would explode at any minute. Summoning up my courage, I gently spoke. "Do you forgive?"

At that, all hell broke loose. "No, no, no! I do *not* forgive!"

My heart started racing. My sister was not ready to deal with this part of her past. I quickly shut everything down and tried to change the atmosphere. I asked Jesus, the Prince of Peace, to fill the car, and in Jesus's name, I commanded any demonic spirit to leave. I quoted the Scripture, "The authority of the name of Jesus causes every knee to bow in reverence! Everything and everyone will one day submit to this name—in the heavenly realm, in the earthly realm, and in the demonic realm" (Philippians 2:10). After that, everything started to calm down.

My sister came back fully aware. I told her what happened and how her face had transformed. She looked at me. "What do you mean, 'my face transformed?'"

I told her, "I saw a spirit that made you look like a pig, and you snarled at me."

She began laughing. "I snarled at you?"

I laughed back. "Yes, you actually showed me your teeth." We drove home, discussing everything that had happened, and she couldn't wait to share the experience with our family. I was kind of freaked out by the whole incident, and so I decided maybe this wasn't the time to keep dealing with my sister's unforgiveness. God, however, had different plans, and He wanted to show her His great love for her.

The day before I was to fly back home, we were getting ready to go to sleep when my sister said, "Aren't you going to pray over me?"

I took a deep breath. "Sure, I would love to pray with you." This time, however, I was going to prepare for a demonic-free encounter. I invited all the angels to come into the room. I then spoke to my sister. "If there are any demons, you will not speak, act, or manifest in my presence." After that, I said, "Okay, let's do this again!"

The Holy Spirit was leading me to minister differently this time. Looking at my sister, I said, "We are just going to do one big prayer of forgiveness. Do you forgive everyone?"

Quickly, she smiled and agreed. I thought, *Perfect, this will be easy, so let's get into this.* I began the prayer by telling my sister how much God loved her.

She simply shook her head. "No, He doesn't."

Chuckling back, I said, "Yes, He does. He is madly in love with you. We just need to get you to see that." I continued ministering as God was moving. "Tina, don't you see God?"

"No, I don't see anything. All I see is darkness."

I replied, "Tina, He's there. God is with you."

She shook her head again. "No, all I can see is black."

I continued praying in the spirit and interceding on her behalf. "God, where are you?"

In my spirit, God said, "Lisa, I'm next to her."

I said, "Tina, God is right by you. Don't you see Him?"

She sighed and frowned. "No, He's not there. It's all black."

Fear crept in and whispered to her, "God isn't coming to save you. He doesn't care about you. He doesn't love you. He wasn't there for you then, and He won't help you now." The little girl inside her felt alone and unloved. But once again, the atmosphere began to shift as her lips quivered and the anger of that little child who didn't think God loved her began to manifest.

At this, I thought, *Oh, no way is the devil stealing this from her*. I used all the Scriptures that I could remember, starting with John 3:16. "For God so loved the world that He gave His only begotten Son, that whoever believes in Him should not perish but have everlasting life" (NKJV). I grabbed her hand and kept shouting verses. "And the Lord, He is the One who goes before you. He will be with you; He will not leave you nor forsake you; do not fear nor be dismayed" (Deuteronomy 31:8 NKJV). I read every Scripture about His love. "The Lord has appeared of old to me, saying: 'Yes, I have loved you with an everlasting love; therefore, with loving kindness I have drawn you'" (Jeremiah 31:3 NKJV). And I read every Scripture that spoke about God claiming her as His. "Fear not, for I have redeemed you; I have called you by your name; You are Mine" (Isaiah 43:1 NKJV).

I was crying out the truth that Tina so desperately needed to hear. The Father was calling her name, "Tinna, Tinnna," a love song calling her to come to Him.

"Tina! God is calling you. Can't you hear Him?" I was pleading for this encounter to become as real to her as it was to me. Then the Father told me to tell her to turn around; she was looking the wrong way. "Turn around, Tina," I cried. "He is behind you."

She turned. "Wait, I see a light. I see it," she shouted without skipping a beat.

"Run to the light!"

Suddenly, my sister's face begin to light up. "I see light." In my spirit, the Lord was calling her. "Wait, I see more light." My jaw dropped at her next words. "I see Him. I see Him!"

She began smiling as she finally stood beside her great love. As the blackness slowly came off her face, it was like watching a movie with the special effects of a computer removing this mask. It was almost like a jigsaw puzzle that was being taken apart piece by piece as the love of the Father began shining on her. Her face gradually became brighter and brighter, revealing His light. "And this Light never fails to shine through darkness—Light that darkness could not overcome!" (John 1:5). Her eyes became clear as the tears were streaming down her face, and suddenly, she could hear and see Jesus.

My sister stood before the King of Kings and Lord of Lords. "Then Jesus said, 'I am light to the world, and those who embrace me will experience life-giving light, and they will never walk in darkness'" (John 8:12). This Scripture became truth as the darkness lifted off her. He washed away all her doubt, fear, and unworthiness as she gazed at Jesus.

In that moment, the Scriptures were coming alive. The Word of God that I spoke was the truth that was bringing her back to her Father. Each passage destroyed the lies that the enemy had spoken to her to keep her trapped in pain. In the Old Testament, Moses's face became brighter when he stood in the presence of God. When Moses looked at the goodness of God, he changed when God's glory came. His face shone, and he covered it because the children of Israel were afraid. (See Exodus 33–34.)

Tina was not only set free, but she saw Jesus. She began asking Him questions as He walked around the room and stood by me. She told me that Jesus was standing next to me and His hand was on top of my head. He was looking down at me with a huge smile like a proud and loving father would look at a daughter. At that time, my sister did not understand the relationship I had with Jesus because I hadn't shared that with her. I was so excited at everything that transpired that night. She could see in the spirit. She drove me to the airport the next day, lighter and more excited than ever before. She had hope for the first time.

I would love to say that after that, my sister completely gave herself to God. That took some time, because a lot of healing still needed to happen in her life. But God would finish the job, because just like the Scripture says, "He who has begun a good work in us will complete it." (See Philippians 1:6.) Four years later, that work would be accomplished. Once again, my sister went through the process of forgiveness. She understood her worth and God's love for her. The layers were all being peeled off, one hurt at time, revealing all the wounds she had buried. After all she had been through, God gave me words of knowledge for whatever I did not know. I used more Scriptures to penetrate the truth of who she was to God: the apple of His eye, His gem, and His precious daughter.

Like a skilled surgeon, God was knitting her back together with His truth. The Holy Spirit was preparing her heart to receive all that He had for her. When we finally finished, we both were crying as she started to realize how much God loved her. She could finally see herself as God's daughter. It was the-woman-at-the-well moment in her life as she encountered Jesus once again, loving her without condemnation. The pain and hurt couldn't stay or have a place in her as love came in to free her.

I told her she needed to get a Bible of her own so that she could start using the Scripture in the same way that I used it when ministering to her. Now that she had a new identity, she needed a new way of thinking. If she started to read the Bible, she would exchange her stinking thinking for a Christlike mind.

I told her I'd go and get her, her very own Bible the next day. I think what surprised me most was that the next morning, she was asking me, "When are we going? Didn't you say you were buying me my Bible today?"

Laughing back at her, I said, "Yes, let's go find a Bible bookstore." Due to the pandemic, we couldn't find one, so I just ordered her one online. Within a few days, it arrived, and she took a picture to show me. She thanked me and was so excited that she now had a weapon from God to use to change her life. I thanked Papa for His goodness. He told me a long time ago, that a day would come when my sister and I would be in unity. That day happened because now I was in Jesus and so was she. We became one in the spirit. Tina was set free and began to live a different life because she finally understood how very powerful the Word of God truly is.

The Word of God is powerful because it's alive and moving. Jesus has given us the ability to speak things into existence in the same way Adam did. When we pray, using the truths of God's Word, it's like God is speaking out those words. All creation on earth and in the spiritual realm must obey the Word of God, so when we use His Word, we will see results as well.

Praying the Scripture:

Heavenly Father, I thank you that the Scriptures have been imprinted on my heart. I thank you that the Holy Spirit can bring your Word to my remembrance when needed. Holy Spirit, remind me of the Scriptures that I have read. Call them up when I need them. I thank you, Father, that your Word does not return void. I thank you that if it is written, then it shall be done. Jesus, I thank you that you have shown me that the promises of the Father are yes and amen. Give me the wisdom to speak your truth, and let those words that have been written fall easily from my lips. I give you thanks and praise in the mighty name of Jesus. Amen.

CHAPTER 2

Obedience

This love means living in obedience to whatever God commands us. For to walk in love toward one another is the unifying commandment we've heard from the beginning.

~ 2 John 1:6

Obedience is crucial in the walk of a believer. In fact, the word *obey* is used 170 times in both the Old and New Testaments.[1] God blesses and rewards the obedience of His children. In obedience, miracles took place, and God's will was accomplished.

From the beginning of creation until Jesus, we see that the struggle to obey God and follow His instructions is very real. Each time people in the Bible chose disobedience, the outcome was not favorable. Yet man has chosen time and time again to disregard the word of the Lord: Adam and Eve, Jonah, Saul, and the list goes on. Man has turned on God and paid the price for that.

In the books of 1 and 2 John, we can see clearly that when we obey God, we demonstrate our love to Him. "If someone claims, 'I have come to know God by experience,' yet doesn't keep God's commands, he is a phony and the truth finds no place in him" (1 John 2:4).

Obedience is not only our love for God but God's love for us. God is trying to keep us safe, and obedience to Him protects us. Look at the protection that God provided for the Israelites as they wandered in the wilderness for forty years. One of God's names is Jehovah-Raah, the shepherd who tenderly leads us, loves us, and keeps us safe.[2] When the sheep follow and obey the Shepherd, they will not get hurt.

One of the first things we notice in the life of Jesus was the complete obedience He had to each and every assignment from God. Even as a young child, Jesus followed the voice of his heavenly Father as He was pulled back into the temple after Passover ended. His family realized that He was no longer with them and had to go back to Jerusalem to find Him. Jesus didn't apologize to His parents; instead, He acknowledged whose voice He was obeying. Jesus wasn't being led by man but by God, even at a young age. At that moment, Mary realized that Jesus knew who He belonged to, and she understood that Jesus was only on loan to her.

We may want to control the destiny of our children or the people that we love. But the greatest gift is to give them back to God and allow them to be everything He has called them to be. Each of them has a destiny prepared perfectly by our loving Father. When we let go, we let God do what He needs to do to get them to their promises. Just as Mary learned with Jesus, the people in our lives don't belong to us; they are only on loan from the Father.

I have marveled at the obedience of some of the heroes of faith in the Scriptures. Abraham had a difficult choice to make—leaving everything and everyone you love—yet God rewarded his obedience by making him the father of many nations. Moses was called to lead the children of Israel out of the slavery of Egypt into the paradise of Israel, but he would have to obey and follow God in order to taste the promised land. David had to wait for the transition from a shepherd to a king by totally relaying on God. The seed sown for our Savior came through his family line. Mary surrendered and gave her body to the most High God. She made the decision to obey and deliver the Messiah. She told the angel, "'Yes! I will be a mother for the Lord! As his servant, I accept whatever he has for me. May everything you have told me come to pass.'" (Luke 1:38). You see, her yes allowed God to bring forth the Savior that would save not only His mother but the entire world. God has created us in love with free will and the ability to choose to obey.

Each and every moment of our lives, we can make choices that will shape and form our pathway to destiny. We become like chess pieces on the board of life. With each move, an event happens, and it all depends on the skill of the player. In this vision, God gives us permission to let Him be the one to move the piece, or we can give that permission to the enemy. If we are being defiant, rebellious, stubborn, and unmovable, then we are playing right into the enemy's hands.

When we look at Scripture, we also see the results of not obeying the Lord. For example, God had chosen Saul to become the first king of Israel, but because of his disobedience, the kingdom was handed to another. King Saul was more concerned with the applause of men rather than pleasing God. When he realized what he had done, he tried to change God's mind, but God knew his heart had been turned from Him. Saul lost his kingdom and, eventually, his life. God sent the prophet Samuel to find a king after His own heart, so Samuel anointed David, the son of Jesse, to become the next king. In the book of Psalms, you can see how David consistently obeyed the Lord in love even when it was hard.

In my personal walk, I have seen the rewards that obedience has brought me. I have been blessed beyond measure by answering the call of God. But obedience was not as easy as I thought it would be. I messed up more times than I can count. The Father would show me where I allowed the enemy to try to convince me to settle for the good instead of pursuing God's best. The pulling of the Holy Spirit always led me back to the road of righteousness.

In the times and seasons of discovery, our heavenly Papa is teaching us how to trust Him and follow His directions. The outcome may be filled with uncertainty, but in the process of building the relationship, we begin to trust more and allow God to lead us into the unknown. Just like Peter saw Jesus walking on the waves, all Peter needed to do was ask Jesus if he could come. Jesus invites to do the same each and every time God wants us to partner with Him as we allow the super to overtake the natural.

The first time God asked me to lay hands on someone for healing, He was encouraging me to step into a new way of praying. The nudge came in the twilight hours of the night. I had just come home from an encounter with God at a church service that left me fully undone. I received my prayer language and felt the power of the Holy Spirit and the love of the God of the universe, which left me on the floor, incapacitated.

I came home, fully transformed and fully equipped. The fire of God was burning me up inside. For the first time, I felt fully alive, and I never wanted it to end. Although I was fully awake, I didn't want to wake anyone, so I quietly climbed into bed. My husband had hurt his shoulder and was worried that it would need surgery. We didn't have insurance at the time, resulting in much stress. I was turning over to go to sleep when the Lord said, "Put your hand on his shoulder."

I thought, *Okay, but then what should I do?* I heard no further instructions. I gently laid my hand on his shoulder, trying not to disturb his slumber. An incredible heat immediately came over not only my hand but my entire being. I felt a release of something, although I wasn't sure what it was.

I removed my hand and turned to my side to go to sleep. I closed my eyes, preparing for my dreams to take over, and to my surprise, I saw the brightest light I've ever seen in my life. It was like looking into the sun at noon, but it didn't hurt my eyes. I quickly opened my eyes. My bedroom was completely dark. My mind was racing with thoughts that I couldn't quite process. I dismissed them and shook them off, thinking that my eyes needed to adjust to the darkness. Closing my eyes again, I went from the darkness of my bedroom into the bright light that was filling my vision. Immediately, my eyes sprung back open into the darkness. Suddenly, a quiet filled my spirit as I was drawn back into this light that wanted to fill every dark place in my mind.

That night, I fell asleep in the arms of my Father. He filled me with more illumination than I'd previously experienced. I woke up and wondered if it had all been a dream. But I knew it was real when my husband easily moved his arm. He was no longer wincing or complaining like usual at any and all motion. I smiled as I asked him how he was feeling. His answer was short as he told me he wasn't even thinking about his shoulder because he didn't have any pain. At that moment, I knew he was healed.

God knew the multiple prayers I had prayed regarding not going to any doctors. He understood our financial struggles and the burden that doctor's visits would place on our family. As a good Father, He was going to show me that He was going to provide for all our needs and teach me what I needed to know. I simply had to choose whether I was willing to follow His lead.

I began a slow process of obedience to everything God would tell me to do. I was constantly filled with many doubts as to if I were really hearing God. I had encounter after encounter, pulling me into a new realm of understanding of obedience. I understood what

Jesus told the disciples: that He was only doing what He saw His Father in heaven doing. But at the time, I thought that Scripture only pertained to Jesus. God was going to show me and give me the revelation needed to walk in that same obedience.

For an entire year, God spent time teaching me how to be a daughter. The Holy Spirit gave me visions and highlighted people that needed prayer. My hunger for knowing more and more about how to hear the voice of God increased. I needed confirmation that I was hearing Him and not just my impulsive thoughts. God began to train my ears to recognize His voice.

God was working in me, using me to pray for people in the quiet of my house. I would begin to pray in tongues and picture someone I knew. I didn't understand what I was saying, but I knew that it was coming from God. He began to give me prayer assignments, and people started to text me for prayer. The Lord was confirming each time I correctly obeyed His instructions. I would get a text or call that confirmed what I was hearing and praying.

I would scroll through Facebook and see posts requesting prayer. I learned that God had specific ones that needed my attention. He needed my obedience to partner with His supernatural in order to see the miraculous. Sometimes I would think, *Okay, let me pray for this one.*

That gentle voice would say, "No, keep scrolling." In that instant, I knew that was not my assignment, and I didn't need to do anything. Trusting that you are following the Father's lead can be difficult, and many times, we will discount what we hear. We will try instead to lean on the teachings of individuals who aren't listening to God but are obeying the religious customs they were taught.

God was honest and forthcoming in every instruction He gave me. We would discuss how not to do something but that I should do it the way He was showing me instead. Sometimes, those instructions were very difficult and uncomfortable to follow. I would get nervous, fearing people would think I was nuts, but following those instructions brought miracles and breakthroughs.

I began ministering where it was safe: at churches or with people I knew. When I was sent out into the marketplace, God really began to stretch my faith and my obedience.

I started to work at a cosmetic counter, helping to bring out beauty in women who would come in for a new look. This would become the bridal chamber where Jesus came to meet His bride. I always knew when it would be a consultation versus an encounter. The atmosphere would always shift when He entered the room.

Papa impressed upon me that I needed to deliver the words that He gave me for people. Sometimes I didn't know or understand why God would share certain secrets about others, but I knew the story about the woman at the well. Jesus knew everything about her. She left there forever changed with all her shame removed.

One day, I was working when these women approached me, looking for some makeup. The lady was from overseas and was visiting her aunt, so she wanted to purchase her cosmetics at a cheaper price than she would pay in her country. The aunt left us to get the right items and said she would return shortly. I was listening intently as the woman spoke, trying to determine the origin of her accent. I asked her where she was visiting from, and she replied, "Ireland."

Without missing a beat, the Lord whispered the word "Dublin."

I asked, "What part of Ireland are you from?"

She replied, "Dublin." Now the shock of hearing her answer in my head before she even spoke began to swirl around me. I was still very new at the gifts of the Holy Spirit, and so I dismissed it as coincidence. I didn't know many towns or cities in Ireland, but I did know of Dublin, so I could rationalize what I heard.

We began having a conversation that quickly shifted to the topic of God. I somehow knew that she was Catholic, which, of course, she confirmed. I saw a book in my mind and began to tell her about it. Surprisingly, her cousin had just given her this same book a few days earlier. The conversation flowed with laughter and excitement as I began sharing my love of God and His goodness. I began picking out a foundation for her as she continued chatting about her Christian cousin here in America.

She was here for a reason, sitting with me and having this crazy conversation about an obscure book. That still, small voice suddenly spoke to my heart. *Tell her she tried to commit suicide on several occasions.* This thought shot through me like a lightning bolt, and I was completely taken off guard. I immediately rebuked it, thinking that those thoughts came from the enemy. I continued listening to the woman as she was rattling off a story about how her cousin was talking to her about Jesus. Once again, this still, small voice spoke to me and repeated the request. *Tell her that she tried to commit suicide on several occasions.*

This time, instead of rebuking the voice, I spoke back to it. I replied, *Lord, is that you? Lord, I can't say that. Lord, what would she say?*

For the third time, that still, small voice spoke to my heart, but this time, God added my name. *Lisa, tell her that she tried to commit suicide on several occasions.* Now I knew that this was God. Immediately, I began to pray in the Spirit, trying to transform the atmosphere so Jesus could encounter His precious daughter.

I quietly positioned myself so that I was now looking at her face. I took in her beautiful blue eyes that held hurts and wounds. I gently said, "I need to ask you a question. It's a serious question and a bit personal." Her reply surprised me because she told me I could ask her anything. She trusted me. How in the world could she trust me? She just met me, but I knew who was leading this conversation and who she was trusting.

I took a deep breath, squeezed her hand, and spoke the words the Lord told me. "The Lord has said you tried to commit suicide on several occasions." Her jaw dropped as I then blurted out, "It's because of the abuse you experienced as a child, but it was never your fault." Again, she gasped at my words. She realized that God had been watching. The tears began falling as, once again, I said, "Some days, you think you look beautiful, but you go to the mirror and are disappointed in what you see."

Emotions overtook her as she cried out, "No one knows this. It's like you are in my head."

For one last time, I blurted out, "That feeling of thinking you're beautiful isn't coming from you but from God. He sees you as beautiful."

My breathing slowed as the oppressive spirit lifted. I continued to minister to her as the tears ran down her face. I looked her right in the eyes and told her that I don't know anything but God knew everything about her. She began to share some intimate details of a life broken because of abuse, wounding, violation of trust, and lack of safety. The story was a mixture of tears and trauma, all unfolding as the love of a Father reached deep into her soul.

I listened and prayed, searching for the right words and wisdom to release into her heart for healing. I asked her if I could pray for her, and she looked so very hopeful as she nodded. I began praying for healing, breaking all the trauma, and calling forth her destiny of promises and victory. As I was holding her and trying to comfort the pain, the aunt returned to collect her niece.

I quickly finished up and said goodbye as I wrapped up her purchases. Joy came over her as she waved goodbye. I smiled and began to praise God for His goodness and wiped the tears from my own eyes as this encounter had touched me so powerfully. The woman ran back and hugged me and whispered into my ear, "Thank you." So many truths came from this encounter, especially the power of obedience and trust we need to walk in as His children. God can take our natural gifts and talents and use them to express His supernatural love.

God also needs our obedience to connect us to the right people in order to move us into our destiny. I have learned to listen to the nudges of the Father to go certain places and to reach out to various people. When I started doing my broadcast *Touched by Prayer* back in 2014, I knew that I would be interviewing people. My biggest challenge was that I didn't know anyone to interview except the people in my church, so that is who I interviewed.

God will give you the opportunity to see if you will follow through with what He asks you to do. God gave me a talk show because I asked for one at a prophetic conference; well, I actually asked to be a talk-show host. Within six months of receiving prayer for that opportunity as a talk-show host, *Touched by Prayer* was born. As I began interviewing the people from my church, God wanted to expand my reach.

I was scrolling through Facebook when I saw a post about a book called *The Longest Bridge Across Water* by Jeremy Mangerchine. I'm not sure why this book caught my attention, but it did. I started seeing this book all over Facebook, and finally, a prophet I was following give a rave review about it. Reading the post, I thought, *I want to read that book.*

As soon as the thought entered my head, the Lord said, "Friend request him."

No way, Lord. I don't friend request men, and I feel weird doing it.

Once again, the Lord said, "Friend request him." I sighed and hit the button to request friendship with this young man. As soon as we connected, I started getting his feed and reading his great posts. Some of the posts were of people sharing the enjoyment of reading his book.

I thought, *God, I want to read that book, but I can't really spend money to buy it right now.* Literally, within an hour, an ad posted with an offer to buy the book for ninety-nine cents. I chuckled and said to the Lord, "Well, all right then, I will read it."

I read it within four hours and couldn't wait to write a review. After I posted on Jeremy's Facebook page, he nicely replied. I was telling everyone I knew about this book and encouraging them to get a copy. The Lord said to ask him to come on *Touched by Prayer*, so I sent him a message, inviting him to the broadcast. He immediately responded, and we set a date to chat and discuss the broadcast.

The first time we talked, it was like being with family, almost as if I had known him my entire life. After we recorded the interview, Jeremy suggested I interview a friend of his, a paramedic who was praying and healing people in his ambulance. Once again, interviewing the Praying Medic opened up new doors to more interviews. I have had many other divine setups by God that have led to interviews and, more importantly, great and lasting relationships. To this day, I am friends with Jeremy and consider him like a son. I am so very grateful that I listened to God and obeyed Him by sending a friend request, because that request brought me so many friends that have truly blessed my life.

The love of God is so much bigger than we know, and He is looking for those who are willing to surrender their own will to obey His will. Jesus says, "Those who truly love me are those who obey my commands. Whoever passionately loves me will be passionately loved by my Father. And I will passionately love him in return and will reveal myself to him" (John 14:21). When we throw away all of our agendas and submit to what the Father has asked, we will see moves of heaven like never before.

Obedience:

Father God, Jesus said that He only did what He saw you do in heaven. I ask you to help me be like your Son and only do what you show or tell me to do. Help me walk in obedience. I humble and yield myself to the plans and purposes that you have for my life. Help me respond quickly. Help me be bold in successfully completing everything you ask. I ask you, Holy Spirit, to guide and strengthen me to do what I'm told to do. May every assignment that you give me bring you glory and honor in Jesus's name. Amen.

CHAPTER 3

Personal and Spiritual Relationship

I have never called you "servants," because a master doesn't confide in his servants, and servants don't always understand what the master is doing. But I call you my most intimate friends, for I reveal to you everything that I've heard from my Father.

~ John 15:15

From the foundations of time, God created man and women for one simple reason: relationship. The core of Christianity is not only following Christ but resembling Him in all you do. To be a follower of Jesus is much more than saying words to a rote prayer; it's living the lifestyle. In any healthy relationship, something happens to the individuals: They begin to act alike.

For example, in marriages, the couple might make similar statements or finish each other's sentences. In a friendship, at times, words aren't even necessary, because the individuals can read each other's thoughts. Even in work environments, you can learn how different people will respond in any situation.

As you spend more and more time with God your Father, certain truths become more apparent. The evidence of the overwhelming love He has for you becomes undeniable. "This is love: He loved us long before we loved him. It was his love, not ours. He proved it by sending his Son to be the pleasing sacrificial offering to take away our sins" (1 John 4:10).

The Scriptures tell you that He wants you to come to Him with all your problems. "Pour out all your worries and stress upon him and leave them there, for he always tenderly cares for you" (1 Peter 5:7). God confirms that He calls you a child and knows everything about you. "Lord, you know everything there is to know about me" (Psalm 139:1).

So many more Scriptures speak about the intimacy we can have with our heavenly Daddy. As you begin to build upon that relationship on a daily basis, a familiarity emerges. Suddenly, you find yourself talking to Him about all your hopes and dreams, looking for comfort from Him for all your hurts and wounds, and turning over all your worries and cares to the Author and Finisher of every perfect work.

This beautiful dance of twists and turns of this life assures you that God is leading you. Jesus told the disciples to ask, and it shall be given to you. (See Matthew 7:7.) Once again, this gives you the "Godfidence" to pray to a Father who is ready to listen.

Many times in prayer or intercession, I am using the relationship with people to put a demand on heaven. If I'm praying for my children, I am reminded of the stories of parents in the Bible. In each scenario, a parent is pulling on the heartstrings of Jesus to receive healing for their child.

For example, one mother asked for healing for her daughter and willingly said she would accept crumbs in order to get her prayer answered. "Then she came and worshiped Him, saying, 'Lord, help me!' But He answered and said, 'It is not good to take the children's bread and throw it to the little dogs.' And she said, 'Yes, Lord, yet even the little dogs eat the crumbs which fall from their masters' table'" (Matthew 15:25–27 NKJV).

Her willingness to go to the Master's feet is the type of prayer that shifts heaven, making it possible for God to move. The mother tugged on the heart of Jesus, revealing how she was willing to accept what He was willing to give her. She also reminded Him that the Master allowed the pups to eat the leftovers that fell to the ground. Jesus responds by remarking that her faith moved Him to answer her prayer.

If this woman didn't know Him but knew of Him, imagine how we can approach Him in intimacy because of our relationship with Him. We would not be begging for crumbs; no, we would be invited to sit at the table and partake of the feast. It's all in how we see our friendship with Jesus. Do we come to him as a stranger or as our best friend? The way we approach Him shows the truth of our relationship.

We have read how Jesus was moved with compassion at the death of His friend Lazarus. He loved His friend, yet He allowed him to fall into the sleep of death. Jesus traveled back to awaken His friend, but He had to pull on heaven to release the grip of death.

Jesus arrived at the tomb when all earthly possibility was depleted, but that wasn't enough to move the rock away. It would take more than that for the impossibility to become a reality. It would take a move of compassion to remove the hand of death. Jesus had a solid friendship with Lazarus; he was not a stranger or even a brand-new friend. No, in fact, Jesus had just been visiting with Lazarus and his sisters. Jesus shared meals and memories with Lazarus, so knowing that His friend was sleeping (i.e., dead) was emotional.

As soon as Jesus came to the village, Martha, the sister of Lazarus, confronted Jesus first. In a mixture of grief and abandonment, she asked Him, "Why didn't you come sooner?" No sooner did He answer when she ran to get her sister, Mary. As soon as Mary heard the news that Jesus had returned, she left her house and ran to Jesus, falling at his feet, weeping.

The beauty in this love relationship between teacher and student moved the heart of Jesus. Her grief tugged at his heartstrings as her tears hit the ground. Mary came to Jesus as more than a student but as someone who knew and loved him deeply. The sight of Jesus filled her with a mixture of surrender and sovereignty. Like her sister, Martha, she knew that her brother would still be alive if Jesus had come sooner, but because of her relationship with Him, she also knew that He had to have a bigger reason for not coming right away. Mary had to trust that Jesus was a good friend to her brother, that He was who He proclaimed to be, and that He could turn this untimely death around.

In that moment, Jesus turned to His Father, calling for a move from heaven to initiate the reversal of Lazarus's untimely death. That pull on the relationship between a son and his father destroyed the power of death. The cries through the bond of a friendship, the kinship of a brother, and the interconnection of a father and son united in one cataclysmic prayer and produced a miracle.

So many times, we forget how extremely important our relationships are. I can pray with more authority and power over my children than a stranger can because I am their mother. The prayers of a husband and wife can defeat darkness that is trying to come against their family. God wants to attach His fire to the partnership between heaven and earth and create dynamite.

I have used my relationships to reach the ears of God. Even as a little girl, I knew that He could hear my petition for a miracle. At the age of seven, my relationship with God was tested.

As I mentioned at the beginning of the book, early one Saturday morning, my baby brother got into my father's tranquilizers and ate them, thinking they were candy. This was before the existence of child safety caps. We didn't know what had happened until he came stumbling past us and collapsed on the floor. My older brother immediately scooped him up to rush him to the hospital. It was pure chaos as the adults were jostling about and shoving my sister and me across the street to a neighbor's house.

I was old enough to understand the severity of the situation and possible outcome of losing my little brother. I began to pray as soon as the reality hit me. I began the bargaining phase with God, telling him that I would start being good and listening better to my parents if He would only save my brother. I thought I could change this situation simply by becoming a more obedient child. I knew deep in my heart that somehow, I would convince God to move on my behalf. Even if I had to beg, plead, or bargain, my prayer for my brother would be answered.

A few hours later, my neighbor dropped my sister and me back home. As I opened the door, I didn't sense any sadness. I ran in and asked where my brother was. Then I saw him, sound asleep on the couch. The doctor had pumped his stomach, and he would fully recover.

I hurried over to my sleeping sibling, and with tears of thankfulness, I looked up to God and smiled because I knew that He had heard me. This is one example of how I used the importance of my relationship with my brother to move the hand of God. What I didn't realize was that God was also using this to increase my relationship with Him.

My faith and trust in prayer continued to increase as I grew older. My mother began to recognize the power I had in prayer because of my relationship with God. She saw how quickly my prayers were answered and began asking me to pray for things. I think she was testing me or God to find out if my prayers really worked.

One day, I came home from high school and was approached by both my parents. They received a letter from my dad's company, stating that they were going to close and he would be receiving a settlement of an early pension. We had moved to Florida, and my dad had taken an extended vacation so that we could settle in. This news was completely unexpected, and that extra money would provide added security. I was attending a Baptist church where I was beginning to understand the truths about God. Since I had come out of a Catholic background, my previous knowledge of the Bible was very limited.

I told my parents that I would pray, but I wanted them to give a large offering to the church. This was a challenge to my dad, especially, because he wasn't a generous man. I'm not sure why I presented those conditions as a part of the agreement to this petition, but my father agreed. I proceeded to go to my knees and began praying for my parents to receive the check. My prayer wasn't long or intense, but apparently it worked, because the check arrived the next day.

I completely forgot about this story until God reminded me. I have met people who have a way of praying that moves the hand of God. You probably know those people as well: They seem to have the attention of God to get prayers answered. So many times, I went to friends or family when all I really needed to do was ask Him.

That relational side of God moves mountains and shifts the heavens in prayers. The first miracle Jesus did was initiated because of the relationship He had with His mother. The bond of the family was tested at a wedding, and this bond showed its strength through a simple request. Mary, the mother of Jesus, came to Him and explained that the groom's family had run out of wine, which would cause great embarrassment. The book of John says this:

Now on the third day, Jesus' mother went to a wedding feast in the Galilean village of Cana Jesus and his disciples were all invited to the banquet, but with so many guests, they ran out of wine. And when Mary realized it, she came to Jesus and asked, "They have no wine; can't you do something about it?"

Jesus replied, "My dear one, don't you understand that if I do this, it will change nothing for you, but it will change everything for me! My hour of unveiling my power has not yet come." Mary then went to the servers and told them, "Whatever Jesus tells you, do it!" (John 2:1–5)

What I love about this is that Mary didn't stop or shut down when Jesus wasn't receptive to her plea. She knew her son and trusted He would listen to her request. Was it a look that convinced Jesus to do the will of His mother? What was it that changed his mind from "I'm not ready to do this" into telling the servers what to do? No one knows for sure, because it isn't recorded. I know the power a mother has with her children when she asks them to do something. The honor and love of a son turned the water into wine. A simple petition from a mother's heart shifted the timeline and released the power of love.

In the same way, we are God's children, and He is looking for those who are willing to be the agents to bring change to current circumstances. We can pray from the love we have for people in our lives, asking God for favor. God will also use your relationship with Him, sending you out to the lost and broken as He did with His Son Jesus. The relationship has a value in heaven because Jesus told us, "On the day of judgment many will say to me, 'Lord, Lord, don't you remember us? Didn't we prophesy in your name? Didn't we cast out demons and do many miracles in your name?' But I will have to say to them, 'Go away from me, you lawless rebels! I've never been joined to you!'" (Matthew 7:22–23).

Remember that when Jesus came, He developed friendships and bonds with His disciples. He had a certain level of intimacy with each person he encountered. He called the disciples "friends" much in the same way that God called Abraham a friend. The lasting ties of alliances formed on earth continued to move the hand of God in heaven after Jesus returned to the Father. The time spent cultivating the soil of dependency on the connection of our Creator—not our works—pleases Him.

God loves what we love and who we love. When we pray or petition the heavens on the behalf of someone we love, we need to believe that God will respond. Our Father is so loving that He uses His children that we are in relationship with to pray for us and the various situations we are going through.

I have often sensed that I need to pray for my family or friends, only to find that they needed it. That connection through the Holy Spirit to the Father is all because of Jesus Christ and reminds us it truly is a family affair. Family is important to the Father, especially when it comes to our parents.

One of my best friends, Cathy, knows how God uses me. She has heard all my stories and the crazy God adventures and seen first-hand how God moves in my life. As such, she has trusted me to pray for her family. My love for Cathy is tremendous, and there is nothing I wouldn't do for her. She is a sister to me, and I love her family because I love her.

During the pandemic, severe restrictions were placed on hospitals, and family could not visit the elderly because of the high risk of spreading COVID. It was a very difficult time in our nation to properly care for our maturing relatives, those we love most.

My friend called me for prayer because her mother-in-law, Charlotte, had been taken to the hospital after a fall. After her release, she fell ill a few months later and needed to be hospitalized again. Unfortunately, this time, the diagnosis was grim, and she was only given a short time to live.

I got a text from Cathy, asking for prayer as the family was preparing to say their goodbyes. Once again, due to pandemic restrictions, the family was not allowed to go to the hospital and say their farewells; instead, they had to do a Facetime phone call. This was so devastating to my friend, and she called me to tell me about the last phone call her husband would have with his mom.

I tried to comfort and love her the best I could over the phone. I was so upset I could not be there with her to hold her hand through this nightmare. I told her I was there in spirit and that I was holding her and her family up in prayer. We can speak words that sound super poetic or very spiritual, but in some cases, those words are really true.

I spent my afternoon praying for Cathy, Scott, their kids, and the rest of the family. I was cleaning up the living room when suddenly Papa said, "Pray!" I immediately sat down and began to pray in the spirit. After a few moments, I was in the hospital room where my friend's mother-in-law was lying. I was completely aware of where I was, although I wasn't there in the flesh but in the spirit.[1]

I began speaking to Charlotte and holding her hand as she was struggling to breathe. I told her, "I'm here with you. It's going to be okay." I could feel her fear. Only one of her sons was with her as that was all the hospital would allow. He was holding her other hand, comforting her as best he could. He didn't see me, but Charlotte did. I approached her and said, "You're not alone, and I'm going to be with you."

All of sudden, a huge bright light beam entered her room, the brightest light I had ever seen. The room and hospital bed almost seemed to disappear as the light became brighter and bigger. Jesus then stepped out of the light, offering His hand in an invitation to join Him. Excitedly, I told Charlotte, "Take His hand. It's Jesus, and He has come for you. Don't worry, you will be safe. No more pain and no more fear." Charlotte lifted her hand to take her Savior's hand. Jesus pulled her spirit up out of the bed and took her into the light. I told her that I would tell her family that she was safe, and suddenly, I was back in my living room. Tears were streaming down my face after the powerful experience I had just witnessed. I saw someone I love enter eternity, and now I needed to share it with her family.

I began thanking Jesus for allowing me to see this tender moment and allowing me the honor of helping Charlotte transition into heaven. I knew that her family was heartbroken at her passing, especially since they weren't present. God heard their cries and answered their prayers because He loved them. He sent me so she would not be alone in the spirit as she took her last breath.

I texted my friend the minute I began to pray, and she texted back a few minutes later that Charlotte had passed. I called to comfort her and to tell her what I had witnessed. I explained how Jesus entered the room through the bright light and how her mother-in-law took His hand and walked into eternity with Him. She was comforted by all those details, and she thanked me for praying for her. I told her to please tell her husband and children how very sorry I was for their loss.

I hung up and thought how wonderful our heavenly Father really is. He knows how to comfort us in our greatest hour of grief, sending hugs and words to let us know that those we love are with Him. We will carry the relationships that we form on this earth into heaven. I look at all the very special people in my life and know we will be together for eternity. How awesome is that!

Relationship:

Heavenly Father, I thank you for the relationships that you have put in my life, and I ask you, Father, to bless them. Help me see the relationships that you have with others through your eyes. I thank you that you've placed people in my life for a purpose. I thank you for giving me authority to pray and intercede for my relationships. I thank you that as you call me to pray for your children, I will see them how you see them and according to the relationship you have with them. Help me position my heart properly as I pray for those you place in my life.
Wash away any judgment I may have and keep my heart pure as I pray for your will to be done in each and every situation. In Jesus's name. Amen.

CHAPTER 4

Faith and Trust

And without faith living within us it would be impossible to please God.
For we come to God in faith knowing that he is real and that he rewards
the faith of those who passionately seek him.
~ Hebrews 11:6

As I reflect on my life about what came first, faith or trust, it reminds me a lot of the famous question with no answer: "What came first, the chicken or the egg?" One could not exist without the other. The truth is, they are a package deal, because without faith, it's impossible to please God, but how can you have faith in God if you don't trust Him? I called on the name of Jesus to rescue me, and I never doubted He would come. As I cried out for my Red Sea moment when all seemed impossible, God showed up and parted the waters of inconceivable odds in my favor.

Although I was not well versed in the stories of the Bible, I had an inner understanding of the goodness of God. I never believed He was bad, and because of that, I had the faith to see His goodness.

As I became a reader of the Word, I started to see that many great men of faith all had to have that same trust in God.

The definition of *trust*, according to *The Merriam-Webster Dictionary*, is "assured reliance on the character, ability, strength, or truth of someone or something."[1] According to the same dictionary, one way *faith* is defined is "belief and trust in and loyalty to God."[2] The Bible, however, has its own definition of faith. "Now faith brings our hopes into reality and becomes the foundation needed to acquire the things we long for. It is all the evidence required to prove what is still unseen" (Hebrews 11:1). This is the first verse of the Hall of Fame chapter in the Bible that describes the heroes of our faith. As you can see, those biblical heroes all had to trust in a living God who would bring their hopes to fruition.

For example, Abraham had profound trust in God and left behind his whole family to follow the Lord to a new location. He took his wife, Sarai, and his brother's son Lot to establish a new life with a new covenant. This type of trust would begin to increase the faith that would become part of the pillars of establishing the relationship with God.

Abraham had faith to allow his name to be changed and to see his barren wife deliver the promises to a lineage filled with descendants that would equal the grains of sand. "And I will establish My covenant between Me and you and your descendants after you in their generations, for an everlasting covenant, to be God to you and your descendants after you" (Genesis 17:7 NKJV). That is why Abraham is considered the father of faith. He would pass on this faith and trust in God to his son Isaac, who would pass it on to his son Jacob. Such great faith and trust were established with the Lord that Abraham would be named the God of Abraham, Isaac, and Jacob. The association of the names from these pillars of faith gave people who didn't know this God an idea of who He was.

We see the faith of Moses who encountered the Lord at Mount Horeb, the mountain of God, and followed orders to deliver his people out of slavery. Although he was created for his calling, he still didn't know the angel of the Lord that was in the burning bush. When God spoke and told Moses who He was, we can see the trust that was established through the covenant of Abraham. Moses would pick up his staff and embark on a journey of friendship and trust. Each time the Lord would tell Moses about the plagues He was planning to send on Egypt, the faith and trust increased. It came to a point where Moses had such complete confidence in whatever God said that he refused to go anywhere without Him.

So many stories in the Bible recount faith and trust in the Lord. We are still encouraged today when reading these: the victory of David killing Goliath, Elijah calling down fire from heaven, the catching of fish by Peter, and, of course, the resurrection of Jesus. The demonstration of each act of faith reminds us that God will move as long we keep our eyes fixed on the Great I AM.

My faith would be stretched so that I, too, could walk in the miracles of the Bible. I didn't understand the supernatural realms of heaven, but I was convinced that God could do anything. My childlike faith would be put to the test when I received a phone call that changed everything.

One morning, at seven o'clock, my cousin called, yelling in a panic that our grandmother's house was on fire. I could hardly move as my brain tried to register this information. My parents were visiting my grandmother and staying at her house, so my dread escalated. My cousin told me to turn on the television. I quickly grabbed the remote, turning the channel to our local news. The helicopter reporter hovered over my grandmother's house as I watched it burn.

My cousin told me that someone was still trapped in the house. I stopped listening and went numb. My husband snatched the phone from me. In an instant, before anyone said anything, I knew it was my mother. I began shouting, "It's my mother, isn't it?"

He calmly spoke to my cousin with short words: "okay" and "yes." I had a vision that she was in the house, and I began to pray. My husband then asked, "Are they are going to airlift her, then?"

My eyes filled with tears. "It's my mother, isn't it?" My husband finally nodded.

I crumbled to the ground and began weeping as he finished the phone call. My heart was racing as I called out to God, "Dear Lord, please don't let her die!" My husband told me to calm down and relayed all the information that he knew. I got up and began to dress as quickly as I could to race to the hospital. My father and grandmother were being taken by ambulance to the emergency department as my mother was being airlifted to the burn unit in the same hospital.

At the hospital, I met my younger brother in the waiting area. I asked to see my father and my grandmother. We were escorted first to my dad's room. He was blackened from the smoke and soot of the fire. He had scrubs on because all he had on when the fire broke out was his underwear. Fear and unbelief were piercing through his steely blue eyes. The tears quickly came as we embraced. I began asking him what happened and where Mom was. He was crying as he blurted out, "I tried to get to her, but the fire was so hot, and I couldn't see."

The nurse came into the room as he was explaining the timeline of the fire. We could now see my grandmother. I walked into her room —she was completely unscathed from the fire, but evidently confused and frail at all she had witnessed. In her broken English, she began to cry in fear as we explained her daughter was being airlifted.

I tried to piece together how everyone else at the house was okay, yet my mother was not. My mom got everyone out of the house as the fire began spreading from room to room. Right then, she realized that her pocketbook with all her money was still inside. She thought she could dash back in for it. She knew the outlay of the house so well that even in the dark, she would be able to navigate it. Or so she thought. The heat and smoke quickly overwhelmed her, and she became disoriented. Instead of exiting the front door, she walked into the bathroom where she became trapped. Smoke began to fill her lungs and pulled her down to the floor where she lay unconscious until the firefighters rescued her.

The entire story was like a bad dream. I couldn't wake up. Medical professionals were assessing her situation and caring for her, putting her into a medically induced coma due to the severity of her injuries and her pain. But as soon as I could see her, the nurse would let me know. She was suffering from third- and fourth-degree burns over 50 percent of her body and had suffered severe smoke inhalation. The prognosis was very grim indeed.

I tried to be strong as the news of her condition devastated my father and brother. I told them to go eat as I waited for my other siblings to arrive. My world was crashing down around me as reality was slowly sinking in. I might lose my mother. I had a very complicated relationship with her, and although I loved her, I didn't like her very much. I had anger from childhood and even adult wounds that could easily allow death to take her from me without a fight. I was going to let her go, and God knew it too. My relationship with my mother-in-law was deepening, and I decided she could give me maternal love from now on. I began to pray, but I wasn't sure how to pray for my mom to die. I didn't want her to suffer, and with such severe burns, I knew that she would not want to live.

A few hours later, we were allowed to go into the burn unit to see our mother. We would need to go two people at a time. My siblings, my cousin, and a few family members were all gathered in the waiting area. My father and I were the first to go in. Each visitor needed to have special attire to enter the sterilized room in the burn unit. We needed to wash our hands and put on gloves, a mask, a hair covering, shoe protectors, and a robe to keep all germs out.

We got ourselves dressed and prepared to enter the room. The nurse assigned to my mom met us as we went in and discussed what we would encounter. As gently as he could, the nurse shared the grim report of her injuries. She had mostly fourth-degree burns on her back, thighs, and legs; third-degree burns on her hands and buttocks; and second-degree burns on her head. She suffered severe smoke inhalation and was intubated to assist her breathing. She was experiencing massive swelling due to the burns, so she was wrapped in gauze. The next twenty-four hours would be critical, and we would be lucky if she made it through the night.

I entered the room and gasped. This blown-up mass looked nothing like my mother. I held my daddy's hand as we approached her. Despite her coma, the nurse told us we could still talk to her because she would hear us although she couldn't respond. I tried to pull my strength together to let her know we were there and to encourage her to fight to come back.

My dad began weeping quietly in the corner as I looked for a place to touch her to let her know I was there. The only part of her I recognized was her feet. I began gently stroking her ankle and foot. I wept as I poured out my love on my mother's feet. That image was so powerful and profound as I reflected on the story of Mary wiping the feet of Jesus with her tears.

I began telling her we were all there. My words of comfort were a declaration of victory over her life. I didn't realize that I was prophesying over her body with the promises God had for her. Peace began to slowly fill my heart as the words fell. "Mom, you are going to get through this."

We left the burn unit and decided to attend the Catholic Mass taking place in the hospital. The service had already begun as we looked for seats. The place was standing room only, so we found a spot in the back corner. I began to weep and cry out to God to heal my mom. I told the Lord that I still loved and needed her. Immediately, a still, small voice spoke to my heart. "Lisa, you need to forgive your mother. You can't pray for her if you haven't forgiven her."

I fell to my knees and asked God, "Please help me forgive so that I can pray for her." A strange peace begin to fill me. God was hearing me, and I also had a part to play even though I didn't understand it. I began to cry again as a new determination of victory overwhelmed me, a determination for my mom to come back to us. This time, I had confidence that God would walk this out with me.

As soon as I got home, the Lord impressed upon me to write a letter to my mom, forgiving her for all the disappointments, hurts, abandonment, and abuse I endured growing up. Surprisingly, I quickly remembered all the incidents that occurred throughout my life. I wrote it all down as the memories came flooding back. When I finished, I looked down at the long, tear-stained letter, releasing my mother from everything. The Lord said to read it aloud and then burn it. My voice began cracking as I started reading the letter out loud to myself. Tears of forgiveness broke each offense so that it was no longer attached to my mom. This beautiful and cathartic act was all done in love and orchestrated by the Father. Once finished, I took the letter and brought it to my kitchen sink. I took a lighter and began burning up all the accusations and hurts and wounds and abandonment and rejection and abuse—all of it—and watched it all go up in flames. I dropped it in the sink in case I needed to extinguish it with water. I smiled and inhaled deeply, knowing that it would be okay.

For the next six weeks, my mother had to endure seven skin graft surgeries. The doctor was hesitant to do the first surgery because of the extensive damage to her lungs. We told him that we knew the risks but God would carry her. As each surgery came, my father and I stood together, declaring she would survive. Faith and trust were building in us as we saw victory, surgery after surgery. We also went to a friend's church where the pastor prayed for my mom. The pastor's wife began praying and then started telling my dad and me that not only would she be healed but that the scars wouldn't be visible. This was my first encounter with a demonstration of the gift of prophecy. As the words fell from her lips, tears began to fall, as God was speaking through her. I tried to capture every sentence that she spoke and hold on to it to remove any lingering doubt. In that moment, God was preparing my heart for the great turnaround that was coming.

I went to visit my mother the next evening. I put on the gown and washed my hands. As I passed the nurses' station, the atmosphere had shifted. The nurses were buzzing with excitement as I entered her room. I took one step in, and my jaw dropped. My mother was awake. Tears began to stream down my face as I slowly approached the bed. My mother was off the oxygen, alert, and smiling at me. The tubes were all removed. She was breathing on her own and wanted to talk to me. The nurse covered the hole where the trachea tube had been inserted. My mother looked at me and said her first words. "I love you." I began weeping as the nurses filled the room. It was as if time stood still.

I replied, "I love you too, Mommy." I asked if I could hug her, and the nurse smiled back with a quick nod. I gently wrapped my arms around her, careful not to touch any of her wounds. I started to share her journey and tried to fill in the blanks. She asked where my dad was , and I told her that he was home with my kids. I told her that we had been praying for her and that God had answered all our prayers and that she was going to fully recover. The nurse agreed and told me that she would be moved into a regular room the next day.

My mom was getting tired, so I gave her a hug goodbye. I couldn't wait to go home and call my siblings with the good news. I shook my head, smiling and crying as I pushed the elevator button. A quiet "thank you" escaped my lips as I looked to heaven. God had kept His promise to me, and my mother would be leaving the hospital soon. The ride home was filled with a joy I had never known before. The goodness of God overwhelmed me. I knew that if God would heal my mom, then He could do anything. My relationship was being shaped and molded into something much bigger than I could ever imagine.

My faith and trust in God were increasing. I was being prepared to encounter Him in new and exciting ways. My childlike faith had been stretched, and there was no going back. The bar had been set, and all God wanted to do now was raise it higher.

I could trust Him with healing and protection, but so many other areas of my life and faith needed to be strengthened—the places with the greatest hurts from friends, family, and those I trusted most. Could I really trust God to be all the names He called Himself? If man could disappoint me time and time again, how could I trust an invisible God to provide for my needs? The church has convinced so many people to never ask God for anything. The Bible, however, speaks a very different truth. In fact, John 14:14 says, "If you ask anything in My name, I will do it" (NKJV).

God knew I had trust issues, and He was about to tear down any wall of doubt about who He is, according to all His names in the

Bible. I knew the Scripture and read about the God who provides but wondered what would happen when push came to shove. At the time, I was listening to all the faith-filled preachers who claimed that Jehovah Jireh was the God of more than enough. They encouraged their listeners to put their faith in the God who could give them a car, a house, or even an expensive watch. These testimonies challenged my religious mindsets as I had questioned those preachers who said I should I take God at His Word.

I needed to transition from a poverty mentality that made me believe I could never obtain the material items I wanted into a kingdom reality of not only having those blessings but also believing that God wanted to give them to me. This would be a process as my childhood was filled with lots of disappointments and empty promises. I came from a middle-class family, so we never seemed to struggle financially, or at least, that was the illusion I was under as a child. My parents never really discussed finances, because my mother took care of them.

But as a teenager, I became aware that we were struggling financially. In addition to that, my mother was an alcoholic. My father would often go and pull her out of bars, and apparently, she didn't want him to interfere any longer. So one day, those two worlds collided, and she choose to leave her family. Unfortunately, not only did she leave, but she wiped out the bank account, taking everything.

My father wouldn't receive another paycheck for two weeks, and we only had a few days of food. My dad borrowed some money, and we ate whatever he could afford. That event created a fear in me, a fear of running out of food that I would carry into adulthood. Any time the funds in our bank account begin to dwindle, I immediately went out and stocked my shelves full of food. I made an inner vow to never allow my children to experience what I had gone through as a teen. Note to self: Never make an inner vow because it will come back to bite you.

At times, I tested the waters to see if God really would provide. I asked for money to pay for bills, unexpected expenses, and rent. I knew in a matter-of-fact way that God would not let me go without. I believed it so much that even my husband-to-be was amazed at how quickly my prayers were answered.

I needed four or five limos for our upcoming wedding and told my soon-to-be husband, Rob, that God would supply the limos. He told me I would have to choose between the horse-drawn carriage for my Cinderella wedding or the limos for the entire wedding party, but I couldn't have both. But I knew God would provide a way. Rob had a video production company and often bartered with his customers. I told him that I would pray for a limo company to contact him and agree to barter his services for the use of limos. Rob smirked. "Yeah. Right. Like *that's* gonna happen."

As soon as he spoke, his cell phone rang. It was a limousine company that Rob had worked with before. It was as if God had listened in and wanted to show up at that precise moment. I chuckled as I told the owner of the limousine company that we were just talking about finding a limo for our upcoming wedding and that we could barter a commercial for their services. Without missing a beat, the owner said, "That's me. I was calling to see if we could barter because I need a new commercial."

Rob looked at me as a huge smile spread across my face. I handed him the phone, and they began discussing the details of the arrangement. I began thanking God once again for His faithfulness. He knew what I needed, and He showed up right on time to give it to me.

Life would throw obstacles in my path, and God would remove them all. He would make a way where there was no way. All the stories of God's faithfulness and my ability to trust Him were teaching me that I would never have to fear. He was continually showing me that He could be trusted and that He would supply me with whatever I needed. God was freeing from an orphan mentality.[3] He wanted me to see myself as His daughter and not a servant. He needed to remove one of the biggest strongholds I had in my life so that I could fully trust Him.

At times, finances fluctuated from month to month since we had our own business. I could keep ahead of the gap in paychecks by buying extra food and storing up essentials so we wouldn't run out of anything. From time to time, God would address this with me. Sometimes, the checks were delayed, and I began to panic. I knew that God would take care of me, but I struggled to fully let go enough to trust Him.

After I was filled with the Holy Spirit and praying in my heavenly language, God began to open up the wound from my teens. He knew that hoarding food so I would not run out was a very sensitive area. As a good Father, He started by using the Scriptures and the stories of the Israelites living on manna from heaven. (See Exodus 16.)

This angelic food kept the Israelites free from sickness and sustained them completely. Each day, they were told to go out and collect enough for themselves and their families. Some refused to believe that God would bring them fresh manna daily. Instead of trusting the Lord, they collected extra, trying to store it in a jar. But later, the manna spoiled and became infested with maggots.

God was helping them have faith to see that He was their provider. He was training them by showing them the error of their ways. Each day was a stretching of their faith and trust in the Lord God Almighty. Yes, God would provide when something came up, but would He do it on a daily basis?

Not only did He feed them in the wilderness, but starting with Joseph, in times of famine in the Bible, the chosen people were fed. The prophet Elijah endured a famine and then a three-year drought. The Lord sent him to a brook for water and had ravens drop bread for him. God seemed to provide everything Elijah needed, but one day, the brook dried up. God told Elijah to go to Zarephath where he would find a widow who would feed him.

So he went to Zarephath. As he arrived at the gates of the village, he saw a widow gathering sticks, and he asked her, "Would you please bring me a little water in a cup?" As she was going to get it, he called to her, "Bring me a bite of bread, too."

But she said, "I swear by the Lord your God that I don't have a single piece of bread in the house. And I have only a handful of flour left in the jar and a little cooking oil in the bottom of the jug. I was just gathering a few sticks to cook this last meal, and then my son and I will die." (1 Kings 17:10–12 NLT)

It was a divine setup to show not only Elijah but the widowed woman that the God who provides could do it even with the last bit of food. Like the widow, it was time for me to begin to understand what lengths God would go to, to break any doubt the He would meet my needs.

Just like Elijah's brook, suddenly, all the finances in our home began to dry up. Every area of income was slowly disappearing. My husband continued to work; however, those invoices were not being paid. Everyone seemed to be going through a dry spell, and we were feeling the heat as the bills kept piling up. I was praying more and believing that God would provide for all our needs. My knee-jerk reaction to go to the grocery store and stock up was thwarted because all our savings were gone. The frustration of knowing that funds were coming but of being unsure of when put a serious strain on our marriage. We seemed to be headed for financial disaster as the days became weeks with no income. In addition, our surplus food was now being depleted.

After more than a month, we were still hearing the check had been sent or it was being processed. We were down to our last box of pancake mix, and I felt like that woman at Zarephath. My husband told me that his brother was coming over after work to get help with his computer. Immediately, a rush of fear overwhelmed me. I thought, *I can't believe it! What am I going to do? We don't have any groceries in the house. And I can't even cook him a meal.* I told my husband to make sure his brother came after dinner to avoid any humiliation. I began to pray again, this time, crying out to the Lord on behalf of my children. As clear as day, I heard in my prayer time, "You and your children shall not go hungry." I immediately jumped off the couch and ran to tell my husband what I had heard.

Rushing into the bedroom, I burst out the news. "We are getting the check today. I heard God say that we would not go hungry, so we are getting the check today."

My husband said, "Are you sure you heard from God?" I couldn't even speak but could only nod my head. The anticipation of the mail truck coming that day was removing all the disappointments of the last six weeks. The motor of the mail truck vibrated in front of our house, and I immediately scrambled to grab the mail. My husband came out as I was looking for the check.

I quickly thumbed past all the bills and junk mail for the check. But it wasn't there. My heart dropped. My husband asked, "Where is the check?"

I shook my head in utter disbelief as I muttered, "It's not here."

My husband began yelling. "You said that God told you the check was coming today! So where is it?"

Again, I quietly replied, "I don't know. God said that me and my children would not go hungry, so I assumed that the check was coming today." That was all it took for the enemy to begin to put doubt back in. My head hung low. I trudged back to the house with tears falling that God had not shown up this time.

My husband's eyes flashed as he cursed. "You know that God is not talking to you. It's your imagination, Lisa. You really need to stop all this silliness. People will think you're crazy."

I began praying again, crying out to God. "Are you really speaking to me?" Before God answered, one of my girlfriends called, asking if I was okay. I began to tell her what was going on, but she stopped me and told me that she would take me out for coffee so that we could talk. I agreed to go out with her after dinner. I figured my brother-in-law would be arriving around the same time, so I could leave.

I cleaned up after dinner, still shaking, and began to get myself ready to be picked up. So many necessities were falling through the cracks due to our financial situation, including coloring my hair. I tried to make the best of it, but it was becoming more difficult. The roots of my hair were very grown out, and I began to weep again. I cried, "Lord, I don't even have money to buy a box of hair coloring!"

I stopped my mini pity party and found a hair clip. I twisted my hair into a bun, washed my face, and took a deep breath as I left the bathroom. Right then, the kids came running to get me. My brother-in-law had arrived, carrying with him bags and bags of groceries. He brought them in and placed them in the kitchen. We told the kids to go out and help carry in the rest of the bags from the car. Once again, I saw the goodness and the faithfulness of my God show up.

Looking up, I quietly thanked God as the tears welled up. I didn't understand why or how my brother-in-law knew about our situation. I discreetly pulled my husband aside and asked him if he had asked his brother to buy groceries. He shook his head no and said that he had only told his brother to eat before he came over. I just looked him in the eye and said, "God told me that we would not go hungry, and we won't!"

My friend pulled up to the driveway, and I quickly grabbed my purse as I headed out the door. I still had tears in my eyes as the grocery bags were still being brought into the house. My friend asked, "What's going on?" I shook my head and told her that God just showed up. She asked me where I wanted to go for a cup of coffee.

I shrugged my shoulders. "Wherever you want to go."

We decided on a diner nearby. We pulled out of the driveway when she looked at me and said, "First, we need to stop at the drugstore and get you a box of hair color."

I told her, "No, I'm fine," but she insisted. She went on to tell me that God had told her to do it as she was driving over to get me. God had told her at the exact moment I was crying out to Him. He heard my despair and immediately responded. God wanted me to know beyond a shadow of a doubt that He would be faithful to provide all my needs.

God knows everything about us and knows our every need. It still surprises me that those silly prayers or conversations that we don't think matter really do. God heard my cries even though I tried to push it off and deal with the disappointments of life. My heavenly Father wanted to let me know that He was listening to my problems and He was solving them. "Turn to me, for my problems seem to be going from bad to worse. Only you can free me from all these troubles!" (Psalm 25:17).

Trust and Faith:

Heavenly Father, the Scriptures say that we all have the faith of a mustard seed. I ask you, Lord, to water that seed to help my faith and my trust in you grow. Lord, please expose any place inside me that has any doubt or fear. Remind me that you are faithful and you will do what you say. Help me see you not as man but as a God who does not lie. Lord, help me trust and believe everything that you have said. Help me stand with boldness and confidence that if I speak to the mountain to be moved, that it will surely move. Fill me with a boldness and a strength that will help me stand when I come to you in prayer. Thank you, Jesus, for being that belt of truth that girds me and holds me tight to see you move in my life. Remind me to use my shield of faith to block the fiery arrows of doubt so that I can achieve victory when I speak. Thank you, Father, that you have given me the necessary tools to get my breakthrough.
And I give you all the glory and honor, in Jesus's name. Amen.

CHAPTER 5

Identity: Daughter-ship and Sonship

For the Holy Spirit makes God's fatherhood real to us as he whispers into our innermost being, "You are God's beloved child!"

~ Romans 8:16

In the beginning, God created a son and daughter to have a relationship with Him when He formed Adam and Eve. He wanted to create a family that would expand and allow him to be a loving Father to each generation. At the fall of man in the garden of Eden, the separation of man and God began. No longer would God allow them access into His garden of provision and fellowship. Adam and Eve would feel the sting of shame, fear, and separation from their Creator.

God still communed with man, although the intimacy of a father-and-son relationship was severely altered by the wages of sin. At the fall of man, a door was opened that allowed unrighteousness to enter so that Lucifer could walk freely through. After the sin of man, a veil formed, separating God's holiness from the iniquity of their disobedience.

After years, God and man would rebuild trust to heal the deception of the garden; in another garden, Jesus the Son would choose obedience over defiance. He came to reinstate the relationship and bonds of God the Father to His children. Jesus claimed His identify as the Son of God. He made no apologies for who He was and His relationship with His Father. The Pharisees, the priests of Israel who should have known Jesus the best, misrepresented His Father. Throughout His ministry, Jesus was teaching the Israelites how to come out of a slave mentality with the goal of turning them into true sons. Jesus addresses this issue head on. "'I speak eternal truth,' Jesus said. 'When you sin, you are not free. You've become a slave in bondage to your sin. And slaves have no permanent standing in a family, like a son does, for a son is a part of the family forever. So, if the Son sets you free from sin, then become a true son and be unquestionably free!'" (John 8:34–36).

Jesus spent time with all of His disciples, showing them the heart of the Father. He represented what it meant to be a son. He planned to bring the sons back to the Father by teaching those closest to Him to model the behavior he taught them.

After the fall, God began to rebuild the broken strings of the disconnection between man and Himself. He needed to rebuild trust, obedience, faith, friendship, and finally, His role as Father. He set new boundaries and established a separation from the surrounding wickedness. The wages of sin would result in death, but God had created man to be with Him for eternity. A plan was set in motion before sin ever entered the picture. That plan would act as a hidden door, revealed in due time, to allow man access to the Father's presence.

God removed a majority of the wickedness before it could compromise man and change his original design. Through the great flood of Noah, the first cleansing of the bloodline began. The lineage of Abraham, Isaac, and Jacob built new and trusting relationships. A loving God clearly showed His faithfulness as each generation overcame adversities. The children of Yahweh would once again be separated from Him as they became slaves in Egypt to both Pharoah and the Egyptian gods. But again, He had a plan to deliver them through Moses. This time, a definitive separation needed to happen between those who would follow the Lord and those who would not.

The crossing through the Red Sea was both a miracle moment and another marker in God's redemptive plans. Moses brought the Israelites out of Egypt and away from the worship of false gods into the wilderness to discover their true God. In the wilderness, they would encounter the God of Adam, a real father. They would learn to see Him as their provider, defender, healer, redeemer, and faithful creator. He would continue to build on the blocks of the new, purified foundation, increasing their faith and trust in God.

It would take a shepherd boy named David to truly learn the heart of God. This transformed man's understanding of his divine purpose: to develop a loving relationship with a relational God. Jesus would then take all these strands of the healed relations from God and knit us back together to our heavenly Father. When Jesus displayed His love, compassion, forgiveness, and miracles, He showed us the truth about the character of the Father. He came as a true representation of who God was and wanted to be to His children.

The crucifixion of Jesus opened the veil so that man could house the Spirit of God. In the same way that the Holy Spirit fell on Jesus after His baptism by John the Baptist, the Holy Spirit fell on man at Pentecost. As soon as they were filled with the Holy Spirit, the apostles began acting like Jesus with signs, wonders, and miracles.

We were created in God's image, according to Genesis. "Then God said, 'Let us make human beings in our image, to be like us. They will reign over the fish in the sea, the birds in the sky, the livestock, all the wild animals on the earth, and the small animals that scurry along the ground'" (Genesis 1:26). As we begin to understand that we are all truly His sons and daughters, we will shift the earth back to the dominion we were given at the foundation of time. This has been a very hard concept for many to comprehend, let alone embrace. How do you transition from a servant mentality into a son–daughter reality? God always has a plan.

Even though God had answered many prayers for me and had been so faithful, I didn't see myself as His daughter. It wasn't until I read the book *The Shack* by Wm. Paul Young that I understood what it was to have a real relationship with God.

That book showed me something different that the church had never shown me before: the personal way that Papa God cared so very much about having a deep connection with man. I was being drawn into the Father's heart through this fictitious story. My heart leapt as, page by page, the unveiling of His endless love was poured out to this broken individual. As I finished the book, I made a decision to find this God that touched my heart so deeply.

As much as I wanted to find this personal God, He wanted me to find Him too. I was clearly hearing His voice more than ever before. He was talking, and I was listening. The Scriptures were slowly coming alive before my eyes. I began to understand a deeper meaning in the stories of the heroes of faith. God was changing my perspective from seeing myself as His servant into seeing myself as His friend. I now had a real relationship with the Creator of the universe.

God began speaking of places I would be traveling to with my family. He was preparing me for encounters that would leave me in awe and wonder. God told me that I would go to Hawaii, and He arranged the trip. In Hawaii, the conversation changed from a sentence to a dialogue. He began conversing with me about His creation, almost like an excited child, showing off their latest accomplishment. I then had to ask myself, *Is this really God, or have I gone insane?*

In my teens, my mother had these conversations with God. I thought, *Is she losing her mind?* Later, she had a breakdown and turned away from God. I didn't want the same fate, so I listened very carefully, trying to weed out anything that would pull me away from Him. In Hawaii, I seemed to hear God more clearly than I could at home. He discussed what He created, how He loved nature, and anything else on His mind.

I was learning that God wanted to talk to me about the little things in life. I always thought that God would only speak to me about the serious situations. I mean, who knew that He loved trees? These conversations didn't stop when I left Hawaii—no, they kept increasing. God was building a solid relationship with me, just as you would with a new friend. He wanted me to trust Him and to show me that trust was mutual. I had no idea why God wanted to build this friendship with me, but I was more than happy to engage.

The conversations were short at first, a few words here and there. As I tuned in more to what He was saying, the conversations became longer. One day, I stopped wanting to do life my way. I was ready to give it all over to God and give up full control of my anger, fear, thoughts, ideas, passions, dreams, and destiny. In letting go, I was actually letting God have His way in all aspects of my life. At the time, my life was falling apart at the seams, and I could not stop it. I had no more fight left. This full-on surrender brought about the most significant change.

My finances, marriage, relationships, children, and reputation were all falling down like a house of cards. It was as if God were allowing the enemy to pull out the pieces of my Jenga tower until it finally collapsed. Years later, I would realize how limited my knowledge was of His goodness. God wanted to restructure how I saw myself physically, emotionally, and spiritually.

After I got baptized in the Holy Spirit and received my spiritual language, my conversations with God intensified. Anything that hindered me from speaking to God was now removed. My prayer language began unwrapping a new depth of interaction between the Lord and me. This new way of conversing opened up both my hearing and my spiritual eyes.

I began praying for hours, intently listening as my heavenly language was developing. I listened to teachings on speaking in tongues and discovered that many believers prayed for hours on end. I really enjoyed this new form of communication and found myself praying almost constantly throughout the day. My friendship with the Holy Spirit was growing as I turned my attention and focus on allowing Him to release new words into my spiritual vocabulary.

I was slowly maturing as a daughter of the Most High God. I had a new language, a new understanding, eyes that began to see into a spiritual realm, and a deeper connection with my heavenly Father. I would see visions of myself in certain places in my house and would know that was where the Father wanted me to go. Reading the Bible became new as I was led to certain stories. I was replacing those old wineskins with the new.

As much as I heard and encountered the Lord, I still had some religious mindsets that needed to be removed. God was trying to help me understand that He saw me as His daughter. His voice deep in my heart said, "This is my beloved daughter in whom I am well pleased." I immediately knew that verse. (See Matthew 3:17.) But I didn't know how to receive those words. Didn't the Father say that about Jesus? How could He say that about me too? My heart raced as those words lingered within.

I immediately repented for thinking that I could ever compare myself with His Son. Where could that thought have possibly come from? Did God really see me as His daughter? Was He truly well pleased with me too? I tried to dismiss the thought, but something inside of me refused to let it go. After that, a new seed of identity dropped into my spirit. God began to blow on that seed, growing it deep into my soul, changing how I saw myself. He was showing me I really was His child and He wanted to be my Papa.

I started to see Jesus as not only my Savior but as a role model of how a child of God should live. Jesus walked in miracles during His ministry here on earth. The Scriptures came alive with the new understanding of my new identity. I watched videos and teachings on the supernatural aspects of God. I kept learning more about the spirit of adoption.

I believed that God knew and loved me, but now that I saw myself as a daughter, everything would change. He would speak to me differently. He began calling me His daughter, His beautiful daughter. I listened to new teachings from pastors who all confirmed the difference between seeing yourself as a servant and as a child of the Most High God. Each day, I learned more about walking as a true daughter.

I had a conversation with God while driving to work. I asked, "Lord, what would you like me to call you? Father? Or do you prefer Abba, Papa, or Daddy?"

He instantly replied, "Daddy. You smile when you say 'Daddy,' because you think of your earthly father." I smiled back as He spoke to me. In the same way God had changed the names of people in the Bible, He had me change His name.

Soon after that, my prayer life transitioned into a new level of intimacy. I began asking my Daddy to intervene on my behalf in any difficult situation. My prayers were quickly answered as I would call on His name. It was as if I had His direct line and He was taking my call every time. During my prayers with others, Daddy God revealed that He wanted them to have that same relationship with Him. I explained why we needed to call Him our Father or Daddy. The intimacy in calling Him Daddy was a reflection of our hearts toward Him and how we truly saw ourselves in the kingdom of God.

"Look with wonder at the depth of the Father's marvelous love that he has lavished on us! He has called us and made us his very own beloved children" (1 John 3:1). The moment I was baptized in the Holy Spirit, God began to open my eyes. I had a new revelation of the importance of walking in my identity as God's child, and I wanted all God's children to understand this too. I began to share these truths with those around me.

During a broadcast, Daddy spoke to my heart. "Lisa, my daughters don't know how to be daughters, and so you will teach them." Immediately, I knew that I would have a women's conference called "Daddy's Girl." It was as if a blueprint were dropped into my spirit of what it would look like. When I really knew that God wanted me to have the conference, I started to make excuses.

Daddy will give you a dream and then connect you with the right people to make it happen. I love it! I had a powerful dream in which a minister told me that he would help me do the conference. I knew it was a God dream, but Daddy needed the right person to help with the right interpretation. That soon happened. I was on a phone call with an upcoming program guest, Melody Paasch, who coincidently had the gift of dream interpretation. The minute I began to tell her the dream, tears began to fall. She listened as I unfolded the dream as if it had happened the previous night. My jaw dropped as she told me that God was telling me that He would help me with the conference. She told me, "Now, all you have to do is ask Him when."

I took it to prayer, and a few days later, Jerry Fishman, a pastor and one of my spiritual fathers, called me. "Lisa, when are you going to do your women's conference? If you are waiting for everything to be perfect, you will be waiting a long time. I would like to help you, so I will book the conference under my ministry. You don't have to worry." Tears began to fall as I agreed. The date available was March 17, St. Patrick's Day. I took it. I figured if St. Patrick could raise the dead, I could raise up daughters for the King.

The conference was full of power and changed many lives that day. What I thought would be a single event became a movement of God. God had placed an important calling on my life: helping women and teaching them their identity. My prayers were heard and answered. God had opened the door that no man could open and also enlarged my vision.

The conferences have now gone to different states and more are being added as I am writing this book. I had a vision in 2019 where Daddy God showed me a sorority house on a college campus. He began to speak to me about the relationships formed in a sorority between the women and the bonds that are established. He showed me the house again in a vision, but this time, the letters weren't Greek; they were Hebrew and spelled out I AM. The Father continued speaking to me. "Lisa, these relationships are not easily broken, because they have made a vow to one another to be together. Regardless of where they go, if they meet someone from the same sorority, they instantly bond. My daughters have an even stronger bond because of me, but they don't understand it. The enemy has caused them to fight, compare, judge, accuse, and not walk in unity. I am raising up a new house where my daughters can dwell in love and compassion. You will help me bring my daughters, my bride, back together." I then started to hear various states called out. "I'm from Daddy's Girl Jersey, I'm from Daddy's Girl Tennessee, I'm from Daddy's Girl Florida, I'm from Daddy's Girl Texas." I began weeping as the love of the Father overwhelmed me. He wanted His daughters to be joined together, supporting and cheering each other on.

The vision ended, and within a few days, I got a call to bring Daddy's Girl to West Virginia. A month later, I got a call to come to Florida, and within a year, I had requests to come to other states. God was opening these doors, expanding the gathering of His daughters.

The attacks on identity, especially against women, have reached an all-time high, but Papa is moving to call His children back to Himself. He wants to show them the truth about who they are and whose they are. Social media and television have created a false understanding of purpose and of living your best life. God knows the plans for our lives because He created the destiny based on each individual's identity. The choice is always ours to make, but our Father keeps calling us to walk on the right path that will lead us to our destiny written in our book in heaven.

We are not slaves who have to do anything to gain God's love; we are not servants that have to perform correctly in order to stay in relationship with the Lord. But we are true sons and daughters who do what the Father asks us and serve Him because we love Him. As we see our identity through the loving eyes of the Father, we can enter the throne room boldly, confident that He will hear our petitions.

Identity:

Heavenly Father, I thank you that I have become a new creation and been knitted into your family tree because of your Son, Jesus

Christ. I thank you that I am now seen as your son or daughter. Holy Spirit, bring my spirit to attention to call God my Abba Father.

Papa, thank you that Romans 8 says I have an inheritance because of your Son, Jesus. I no longer come to you as a servant or a slave but as your child. Keep me focused on the truths that you are in me and that Jesus is in me, I am in Him, and we are in you. I am no longer an orphan, but I am your child. Help me understand my authority and help me move as a representative of your holy family. I come out of agreement with any lie that says I am not yours. And I thank you that not only do you see me, but you hear me. I'm so happy that you sent your Son to pull me back into your loving arms. May my life be a testimony that brings others into their identity as your child. I pray this in Jesus's name. Amen.

CHAPTER 6
Names of God and Covenant

*Yahweh says: "When the time of showing you favor has come, I will
answer your heart's cry. I will help you in the day of salvation, for I have
fixed my eyes on you. I have made you a covenant people to restore the
land and to resettle families on forgotten inheritances."*

~ Isaiah 49:8

God is looking to build relationship with us in every area of
our lives. The Lord established a covenant with man
through Adam since the beginning of time. God spoke the word
that created a covenant with all creation, including the sun, moon,
stars, and seas. These foundational agreements gave the earth clear
understanding and boundaries. God also proclaimed that Adam
would rule over the land, sea, air, and all creation because of His
covenant. As such, God established foundational principles for
man's authority and sovereignty over the earth.

When satan entered the garden of Eden, he wanted to usurp the
power and authority of Adam's covenant with God. As soon as sin

entered and man fell, the covenant was now altered. Instead of blessings, curses were added to the contract. God spoke an addendum that both cursed satan and restricted the freedom between God and Adam.

Unfortunately, due to the entrance of sin, God would now judge man because of his disobedience. A new guideline of what God would do and what man would now be responsible to do needed to be established. God's oath or agreement of His willingness to move on behalf of His children makes covenant so important.

God also told Adam to be certain in the covenant of what He was about to do or what Adam could expect. God established two types of covenants: conditional and unconditional. The conditional also established the rules and expectations of what man needed to do in order to keep the covenant. The unconditional covenant or promises were not contingent on anything man did.

The covenants and promises of God are powerful reminders that God wants so much more for us than we think. His promises still hold true even though they were spoken so very long ago.

The redemptive nature of God was to repair the split between Himself and man. He knew that a new covenant would have to be made in order to rebuild a relationship with man. God decided to rid the earth of the seed of corruption that began to produce unrighteousness. Before God flooded the earth, He saved a remnant of the seed of Adam to continue his bloodline through his descendent Noah and his family. After the great flood, a new promise was established between man and the earth. The Lord spoke this new covenant:

This is the sign of the covenant which I make between Me and you, and every living creature that is with you, for perpetual generations: I set My rainbow in the cloud, and it shall be for the sign of the covenant between Me and the earth. It shall be, when I bring a cloud over the earth, that the rainbow shall be seen in the cloud; and I will remember My covenant which is between Me and you and every living creature of all flesh; the waters shall never again become a flood to destroy all flesh. The rainbow shall be in the cloud, and I will look on it to remember the everlasting covenant between God and every living creature of all flesh that is on the earth." And God said to Noah, "This is the sign of the covenant which I have established between Me and all flesh that is on the earth." (Genesis 9:12–17 NKJV)

God set His rainbow in the heaven as a reminder of His promise. The book of Revelation mentions that "there was a rainbow around the throne, in appearance like an emerald" (Revelation 4:3 NKJV). Ezekiel also speaks of that same rainbow. "Like the appearance of a rainbow in a cloud on a rainy day, so was the appearance of the brightness all around it. This was the appearance of the likeness of the glory of the Lord" (Ezekiel 1:28 NKJV).

The rainbow that Noah saw represents the rainbow from God's throne room in heaven. God was showing His rainbow that encircles the throne and thereby declaring this is the highest level of rule over earth and heaven. This glimpse into the heavenly realms is both to remind man and to declare the promise of His covenant on the earth. God once again blessed Noah and the earth, which revealed God's heart for restoration by reestablishing His oath in this covenant of protection. He then went on to bless Noah and his descendants to be fruitful and multiply, increasing man's presence on earth.

The next phase of God's plan was to rebuild his friendship with man, and He did that with Abram. He began by separating Abram from his family, far away from the worship of false gods. This new relationship would begin to form trust and accountability. New roads of promises were being spoken to Abram as his dependency on God grew.

During each encounter with the Lord, God declared more of the plans He had for Abram. God gave him land, granted him protection, declared destiny over him, and established future generations. God prophesied a long lineage over Abram, which was confirmed through the stars at night and the grains of sand during the day. This prophecy began shifting the plans of God into fulfillment as He changed Abram's name, which means "exalted father," into Abraham, which means "father of many nations."[1] As soon as his name was changed, the Lord declared that his wife Sarah (formerly Sarai) would have the promised son, to be named Isaac. (See Genesis 17.)

This covenant, the Abrahamic covenant, began blessings of future generations, giving them more land and increasing God's children. This covenant included Abraham's son Isaac and then his grandson Jacob, blessing all the generations to come.

More covenants later followed that needed to be established. Moses led the children of Israel out of Egypt into a promised land flowing with milk and honey. God would write new laws for the children of Israel to follow, and they would enter yet another covenant. However, this Mosaic covenant would be conditional. As long as they remained obedient to the law, they would be blessed; if they were disobedient, they would be cursed. If Israel was faithful to God, then God would be faithful to Israel.

God would once again walk with the children of Israel through the wilderness and give them back the territory that was taken. The Lord revealed His names through the forty years in the wilderness: His name of healing, provision, protection, and so many more as years passed. These acts of God once again displayed the long-standing oath that He swore to all generations. This Mosaic covenant emphasized the following: God's holiness, the definition and nature of sin, separation from sin, God's constant presence with His children, the importance of love for God and your neighbor, and the depiction of Jesus as the lamb who would take away the sin of the world.

As the Israelites battled in the wilderness for the territory that had been pledged to them, God delivered the victory, signifying the giving back of the land as a blessing that was originated with Abraham and was then reestablished through Moses. The Israelites held tight to the Word of God, and each promise became like a sword in their hands, proclaiming the coming victory. As long as they stayed in complete obedience, the battle belonged to the Lord to deliver them so they would triumph over their enemies.

Each of the covenants and promises were all a precursor leading up to the new and final covenant given through God's Son, Jesus. This was the covenant the prophets spoke about and the fulfillment of all the Lord God had promised. This better covenant wrote the law on the hearts and minds of man. This also fulfilled the covenant or promise that God made to David. The Lord told David that the Messiah would come through his bloodline; Jesus was that descendant born to the virgin Mary.

This is the covenant through which we pray as born-again, Spirit-filled believers. Yet so many Christian believers pray, not really believing that their prayers are being heard. Bible-reading individuals commonly believe that God denied their request because He didn't want to answer their petition. John 16:24 clearly states, "Until now you've not been bold enough to ask the Father for a single thing in my name, but now you can ask, and keep on asking him! And you can be sure that you'll receive what you ask for, and your joy will have no limits!" This is praying using the name above all names and entering through the new covenant, a win-win way to pray. The Father not only hears our prayers, but according to

Jesus, He wants to answer them with an overwhelming yes and amen.

The covenant through Jesus Christ also gives us our adoption papers, so we are recognized as God's true sons and daughters. God wanted to get us back into right relationship with Him. "For it was always in his perfect plan to adopt us as his delightful children, through our union with Jesus, the Anointed One, so that his tremendous love that cascades over us would glorify his grace—for the same love he has for the Beloved, Jesus, he has for us. And this unfolding plan brings him great pleasure!" (Ephesians 1:5–6). We are now His, which was made possible through His Son and the crucifixion.

Through our sonship, we have access to God as His family, just like Adam and Eve had in the garden of Eden. Now that we have access to all the promises of God, we need to be sure that we actually walk in them. "Now the promise of entering into God's rest is still for us today. So we must be extremely careful to ensure that we all embrace the fullness of that promise and not fail to experience it" (Hebrews 4:1). Jesus came to reveal the true heart of the Father and show His nature. We can see the true character and nature of God by what Jesus did.

By using the name of Jesus, we are reminding God that we are in covenant with His Son. In addition, the name of Jesus has a power of its own. Using the name above all names comes with great power and with great resistance. No wonder people get all bent out of shape when you say "Jesus"—the Scriptures back this up. "The authority of the name of Jesus causes every knee to bow in reverence! Everything and everyone will one day submit to this name—in the heavenly realm, in the earthly realm, and in the demonic realm" (Philippians 2:10). There is no name greater than Jesus, and the enemy doesn't want us to understand all that is in His name.

When we pray using the names of God, we also enter all His promises and see the fulfilment of what Jesus accomplished. The Father reveals His nature—who He is and what He will do—through His many names. Jesus came as the Word of God to become flesh as the hands and feet of the Lord. As part of the Godhead, Jesus has many names: healer, provider, light, savior, rock, word, lamb, shepherd, door, bread, and redeemer, to name a few. In the first four Gospels, you see these names pertaining to Jesus and His ministry.

The first mention of God's name as provider is in the book of Genesis as Abraham was given a substitute sacrifice for his son Isaac. Jesus was that substitute sacrifice for man, which is why He is called the Lamb of God. "The very next day, John saw Jesus coming to him to be baptized, and John cried out, 'Look! There he is —God's Lamb! He takes away the sin of the entire world!'" (John 1:29).

Many of His names were divulged in difficult circumstances when God wanted to demonstrate His true character to His children. Each name displays the nature and characteristic of God as a good Father. The Israelites were taught to call upon the various names of God for each situation they encountered. In the Bible, God has introduced Himself using over three hundred names; each name declares a different facet of His identity.[2] In each predicament, God had a new opportunity to introduce Himself in a new way to His children. In this way, those who called out that name were assured that God would respond to their plea. God gave instructions to the Israelites throughout the generations to call on the names of God and pray through the covenants.

The New Testament, however, modeled a better way through the teaching of Jesus. In Matthew 5–6, Jesus taught new truths about the heart of God. He spoke about forgiveness, humility, integrity, trust, faith, provision, honor, mercy, and most importantly, how to pray when He taught them the Lord's prayer. At the Last Supper, Jesus lifts His cup and tells the disciples that they are to drink the wine and eat the bread, binding themselves into this new covenant that was prophesied. The wine represented the blood that would cover all the sins of man, and the bread was the new manna, Jesus giving them everlasting and eternal life.

Jesus established a new and better way as He walked to the cross. No longer would the priests be the intermediary between God and His children. The veil that separated them would be completely ripped apart as the Son of God would be sacrificed to open up the door to communication. Once the blood of Jesus paid the debt, the curse was broken, allowing a complete cleansing of sin. The removal of iniquity gave man the ability to commune once again with God the Father. This purification of the temple of man opened the door for the Father to dwell freely and granted man the ability to be filled with the Holy Spirit.

Each person could now enter the throne room with God the Father because they were going in through the King of Kings. His glory would once again fill the earth as sons and daughters were being transformed into His likeness. As it says in Hebrews,

But as it now is, He [Christ] has acquired a [priestly] ministry which is as much superior and more excellent [than the old] as the covenant (the agreement) of which He is the Mediator (the Arbiter, Agent) is superior and more excellent, [because] it is enacted and rests upon more important (sublimer, higher, and nobler) promises. For if that first covenant had been without defect, there would have been no room for another one or an attempt to institute another one. (Hebrews 8:6–7 AMPC)

I love what Brian Simmons writes in the introduction to the book of Hebrews in The Passion Translation. "All God commanded under the first covenant on earth became obsolete and disappeared thanks to what Jesus accomplished in heaven!"[3] God had planned out everything perfectly, and the book of Hebrews confirms it.

I never thought much about covenant before, but God began to teach me that we have power when we are walking in agreement with Him. We are all His children, and we have choices to make. In the same way that the angels have free will, so, too, does man. God established the law over the earth, and those rules still apply. The most loving offering that God could give to His children was His Son to seal the contract on our lives. His desire is to live with us in eternity and not lose one of His children to sin. The redemptive blood of Jesus washes away the iniquity that keeps God at a distance.

As God's children, we walk in victory when we pray, entering in through our covenant with Jesus and addressing God as we hold tight to the promises that we declare in His name. In each victory, we are leveling up and intimately learning the many names of God. I can list many times when I called on Jehovah Jireh, the God who supplied my needs, or Jehovah Rapha, the God who heals. I also love it when I am introduced to a new name of God during a season of tribulations.

God will begin to prepare your heart when you are about to enter a hard trial. In my time of prayer, I often find He will begin to reveal new truths and understanding of who He is. His many names surface as a sign of help as you begin calling out to Him. God will also remind me of His promises and that He is with me, thus confirming we are in covenant. As the Holy Spirit prompts me to pray, God reveals His name and nature to position me in places to encounter Him.

The first time I ever heard one of the names of God was during prayer. I was praying in the spirit and suddenly began to speak in English. As soon I spoke the words in tongues, without a breath, I began to interpret what was being said in the spirit. I said, "I AM that I AM." God spoke those same words to Moses when he encountered the burning bush. My thoughts were screaming, *It's God, it's Jesus, it's God, it's Jesus,* and I finally settled in my spirit that they are one and the same.

Hearing those words changed everything and helped me understand how real God is. He spoke about what we do together and the plans He had for me. From that day forward, my life would never be the same. The great I AM had spoken—He revealed Himself through His name, and in the same way Moses was called, so was I. The Lord spoke to many in the Bible—Abraham, Joshua, and so many others—why couldn't He speak to me?

The reality that God speaks and I can hear Him changed my prayers drastically. I no longer was talking to air but to my heavenly Father, who was quickly becoming my very best friend. He was teaching me secrets in the Bible as Holy Spirit revealed each truth of who God was. Through those names, my requests were quickly answered.

We don't know some of the names of God, because we have no real need for that facet of Him. Other religions outside of Christianity have different gods. The people worship and offer sacrifices to these gods in an effort to make their prayers heard. Yet, we as believers in Jesus have one true triune God who can meet our every need. In fact, He calls himself El Shaddai, the God Almighty. Ephesians 3:20 states that He "is able to do exceedingly abundantly above all we can ask or think" or imagine (NKJV).

This became my life verse as I became more trusting of the Great I AM. I could see how God was working in and through me as I leaned in closer to my Abba Father. He spoke to me, and I listened, following as He told me where to go and what to say. This new way of conversing with El Shama—the God who hears or listens to my prayers, petitions, and everyday concerns—was very comforting. He both heard and valued every word I spoke. Not one syllable would slip past His ears. This truth comforted me so much as I loved to share my heart and thoughts with the God that created and called me by name. I shared my deepest secrets and desires with Him as I would with my best friend.

The Lord's encounters with the men and women in the Bible remind us how very personal He is. God has been watching all of creation since the beginning of time. He saw everything that occurred in the garden with Adam and Eve. In Genesis, He saw Hagar, the servant of Abraham and Sarah, running away due to the harsh treatment from her mistress. The angel of the Lord found her crying by a spring of water and took compassion on her due to all she had endured. Hagar, who was not an Israelite but an Egyptian, recognized that God had seen it all, and because of that, she names the well she is at Beer-lahai-roi for "the living one who sees me."[4] This is her altar to God, reminding all who drink from this well that God sees us too. (See Genesis 16.) God became more real to me with each encounter I had with Him. I discovered that those encounters with God in the Bible were not only for that time but for today as well.

El Roi, the all-seeing God who saw Hagar, saw me as He spoke to His broken daughter. I was lost and alone, abandoned, and unable to understand what I had done wrong. The Father spoke my name as I curled up in a blanket of tears and emotions. "Lisa, I see you." My mind reeled as He repeated those same words. "I see you." Was God saying that He saw me or that He saw what I had gone through? A short time later, I got a prophetic word that confirmed He saw it all: the battles, disappointments, hurts, betrayal, fear, abandonment, jealousy, and so much more. He didn't turn away from any of it, no matter how bad I thought the situation was or how much of it I was responsible for.

God both see the troubles and difficulties we go through and sees everything and takes notice. The Father was watching Jesus as John the Baptist baptized Him. "And suddenly a voice came from heaven, saying, 'This is My beloved Son, in whom I am well pleased'" (Matthew 3:17 NKJV). I have had guests on my talk show *Touched by Prayer*, who have had near-death experiences. On one broadcast, Randy Kay told me that while in heaven, he watched his life play out before him just like a movie.

In 2016, at a conference with my friend, the speaker told us to listen to this song. We were instructed not to sing along but to simply let the Holy Spirit reveal the love of the Father over us. Celine Dion began to sing "Because You Loved Me." Closing my eyes, I allowed the Holy Spirit to sing this song over me and resisted the urge to sing along.

Suddenly, a movie began to play in my mind in perfect harmony with the words. The movie was about me. I saw myself from a new perspective; the Father was revealing to me that He was watching. I was viewing the images as I prayed for people at my cosmetic counter, held women as they cried, laughed as the joy hit, and prayed as tears streamed down my face—all the snapshots of my life were being played out before me, beautifully assembled by the Creator who was there. The tears of love began falling as my heavenly Father overwhelmed me with approval and validation. The song was coming to its climatic conclusion as Celine gently sang out the last verse about how we are everything because He loves us. The ending was in slow-motion as I was jumping up and down like in a romantic movie with such joy and a twinkle in my eyes. That was how God decided to end this vision. As the image slowly faded, the Father said, "This is just the beginning."

When the song ended, the speaker returned to the front. "Okay, now before you speak, write down what the Holy Spirit showed you." I snatched my notebook and began jotting down the images and scenes of my life that played before me. This touched me so deeply, and I tried to chase away any doubt that this was my imagination. Yes, God not only knew me but saw me! He was watching my every move like a proud papa.

All this was possible because I said yes, yes to following Jesus and allowing Him into my life. I said yes to being filled with the Holy Spirit, who guides and directs my steps. I said yes to God using me however He wants. My yes was signing my name to a contract between God and me. I entered into this agreement, knowing that it would change my life forever. This amazing covenant between man and God is filled with hope, joy, promises, life, freedom, truth, protection, provision, and overwhelming love.

God saw all that happened to me, and He saw what happened to you too. The God of creation has a covenant with His children through His Son, Jesus Christ, which grafts us back into His heart. We get to know Him through the Holy Spirit, and He reveals who He is. We can start building trust with Him in our prayer life, knowing that He will answer us because of the covenant we have in Jesus.

PROMISES AND COVENANT:

Heavenly Father, remind me of all the promises that you have spoken to my heart. Pull back the storms of confusion that have cluttered my mind and reveal your rainbow that the promises are coming. Lord, I ask you to remind me of the covenant that I have made. Holy Spirit, remind me where I may have broken covenant and come out of agreement. Lord, I repent, and I ask you to amend the covenant through the blood of Jesus Christ so that I am in right standing with you. Father, just like all the promises that you gave to the great men in the Bible, you have not changed. I ask you to move on behalf of the covenant that says I am blessed and not cursed. I stand on the covenant that says that I am a new creation in Christ, that the old has gone away, and that this new and everlasting covenant shall be for eternity. Thank you for the promises that you have placed inside my heart. Holy Spirit, thank you for your guidance so that I will see these promises fulfilled. And Jesus, thank you that this covenant has been signed with your blood that will never fade. I give you all the praise and honor, in Jesus's name. Amen.

CHAPTER 7

Prophecy and Word of Knowledge

No true prophecy comes from human initiative but is inspired by the moving of the Holy Spirit upon those who spoke the message that came from God.

~ 2 Peter 1:21

Since the foundation of the earth, God's desire was to communicate with man. He daily met with Adam and Eve in the cool of the garden, according to Genesis. As the corruption of man increased, the willingness to listen to God decreased. God sent His Spirit to reestablish the ability to both know His voice and to know what God was about to do in the earth through the Holy Spirit.

The spirit of prophecy through the Holy Spirit was upon the prophets, kings, and priests in the Old Testament. God chose who His Spirit would rest upon, and God could remove His Spirit just as easily. Genesis 1 tells us how the Spirit of God hovered over the earth, and through Him, life came. The Holy Spirit, otherwise known as the breath of God, brings life to everything. "The earth was without form and an empty waste, and darkness was upon the face of the very great deep. The Spirit of God was moving (hovering, brooding) over the face of the waters" (Genesis 1:2 AMPC).

In the Old Testament, the prophecies spoken by the prophets of God did all the following: offered correction and direction, established the will of the Lord, and brought forth hope for future promises. The ability to speak out declarations from God enabled man to be the vessel for God to have His way. Prophecy became the seed of promises for many children of faith to follow and believe. But many of the prophets in the Bible never actually saw the prophecies about Jesus come to fruition. Even so, God was faithful to fulfill every single one of them.

The testimony of Jesus Christ is the spirit of prophecy, according to Revelation 19:10. Under the new covenant with Jesus, every believer has the ability to prophesy because of the Holy Spirit living inside them. In fact, the apostle Paul suggests in 1 Corinthians 14:1 that we all pray earnestly to have the gift of prophecy. By having the Spirit upon us and within us, prophecy is accessible to all.

There is a difference, however, in the gift of prophecy and the office of the prophet. The gift of prophecy is simply that—a gift from the Holy Spirit—whereas the office of the prophet is a calling from God. Simple prophecy is for edification, exhortation, and comfort. Let's break this down further. Edification is to build up and strengthen your relationship with God. Based on my understanding, the word *exhortation* means to strongly encourage or to give counsel from God. Lastly, we have comfort, not as man gives but as God gives. This kind of comfort brings healing and freedom and breaks strongholds, such as fear. Now the office of a prophet is a true prophet who will direct, correct, warn, govern, and equip the children of God. You may have very accurate prophetic words to share, but that does not mean you are a prophet.

This confusion between the office of the prophet and the gift of prophecy has caused division in the body of Christ. The beauty of prophecy is we can tap into the true heart of our Father. We can call things as He has ordained them and see those things that are a possibility become a reality. Many of His children refuse to accept that prophecy is still for today or even that God still speaks to His children. Although I was a believer since I was sixteen, I had no clue about the gift of prophecy and did not even know what the office of a prophet was.

As a child, I always had such a vivid imagination and felt as if some of the things I saw were so real. I would dismiss the vision until some of them began to happen. I thought I just had psychic abilities like my grandmother. I knew when someone was pregnant before it was announced. I knew the outcome of movies and family situations. I was concerned about my aunt before she was in a bad car accident, and I have many more examples. My family seemed to have that gift, according to my mom. My ancestors on her side of the family had it as well.

Once I learned about the supernatural part of God, everything began to make sense. I had a pull to supernatural movies and books from my childhood, and now I understood why. My heavenly Father created me to be supernatural just like Him. As my under-standing grew, I began reading books and watching teachings from people of great faith, such as the late prophet John Paul Jackson. I spent hours watching videos or teachings of the prophetic and supernatural ways of God. My daily routine as I cleaned was to watch the television show *It's Supernatural with Sid Roth* and listen to the amazing stories about God.

I joyfully accepted the truth that I was created to live a supernatural life. My new life was to spend hours praying in the spirit and communing with God. I prayed each morning with a list of wishes to be filled by God, not truly understanding who He really was. My prayers began to transition as I started to feel the unction of the Holy Spirit specifically whisper in my heart, "Pray for this or that."

As I mentioned earlier, while scrolling through Facebook, a prayer request would soon catch my attention. The Holy Spirit was pulling me to pray in the spirit for that individual and their circumstances. I was shown what to pray, and a few days later, I would see the confirmation of answered prayer. But I didn't really understand what was happening in the spiritual realm or that I was moving prophetically in prayer. I simply continued as the Holy Spirit led me.

One day, I received a text from my friend Dana to pray for her friend Teddy who had recently been rushed to the hospital because a car fell on him while he was changing a tire. Immediately, I began praying in the spirit, not knowing the full extent of his injuries. The Lord said, "He is with me," as I continued in prayer. I shook my head in disbelief and tried to rationalize that it must have been me and my fear coming through. A short time later, Dana texted me again, explaining Teddy's injuries in detail. His body had been crushed, he was in a coma, and they were sure of the outcome.

The next day, some of the neighbors were discussing this tragedy. Another Christian lady believed that Teddy was with God in heaven. It was a confirmation of what I heard, and I exclaimed that I heard the same the thing too.

The news spread, and events to cover the costs of the accident were underway. I continued praying for Teddy, whom I really didn't know, but he was like a brother to Dana. In prayer, the Holy Spirit would specifically tell me how to pray for him, and I would find out later that this was, in fact, a medical issue that needed intercession. I told Dana how God loved Teddy, and he was safe with the Father. I knew in my spirit that he would wake up from the coma and told Dana that this would happen. As much as she wanted to believe this, her trust in God was nil, and she politely nodded to appease me.

However, God was not joking around. I was on my back deck, praying for Teddy, and I could see his hospital room and the bed with him lying on it. At least I thought it was him, because all I could see was a body with the legs under the sheets. The vision was so real, and yet I could still feel the chair that I was sitting on. The wind was blowing my hair around, yet I could not move as I was caught up in the vision before me. The machines were beeping more loudly, and the legs of the man in the hospital bed began to kick wildly into the air. In an instant, people were yelling, and then the Lord said, "He's baack," in a sing-song and dramatic way.

Seconds later, the vision ended, and I was again fully aware of all my surroundings. I shook my head and grabbed my cell phone to text Dana, but what could I say without sounding crazy? I asked if there were any updates; she texted back that they had just moved him to another hospital. I brushed off my vision as confirmation of movement from one hospital to another.

The next day, my best friend, who is also friends with Dana, came by to drop off some coffee for me. As soon as she walked through my front door, she asked me if I had heard from Dana. I told her I had texted her yesterday but had not heard back. She smiled and said that Teddy had woken up from his coma the previous day.

The words hit me like a wrecking ball as I dropped to my knees as if the wind were knocked out of me. I began weeping and praising God. Her forehead furrowed, she offered her hand to help me up. The tears were flowing like a river as I tried to explain what I saw the day before. We pieced the times together, and Teddy woke up around the same time that I had the encounter. I began shouting and praising the Father for His goodness and faithfulness.

I hugged my friend tightly as we both had tears in our eyes. We had witnessed a real miracle. We called Dana and put her on speaker as we shared the experience with her. To this day, I'm not sure if she believed everything we shared about my vision of Teddy waking from the coma. This would not be the last testimony I had of people waking from a coma. The truth that God showed me is if I was willing to pray for people, I would see miracles.

This was how God began to teach me about using prophecy in prayer. He showed me what was possible by using my faith and trusting in Him. If I could see God in any situation I was praying for, I could trust that God would answer that prayer. The interesting thing about prophecy is some of the crazy things that came out of my mouth actually happened.

In 2013, at my first prophetic conference, Randy Clark's Voice of the Prophet, my prophetic gifting really began to open up. The Sunday morning after the conference ended, we were eating breakfast before hitting the road. I was going to get a cup of coffee when I noticed this elderly woman who I had seen getting prayer the night before. I asked if she was healed the previous night. She smiled and shook her head no. Her friend, not her, was being prayed over. I started to share what God was revealing to me about her. Her eyes filled with excitement as the Father continued releasing His love to her. I had no idea that beneath this woman's smile, so much pain was buried.

She stopped me for a moment to ask if she should record all I was saying. I told her that wasn't necessary because the Holy Spirit would remind her. When I got my coffee, she had returned to her table and was sitting alone, writing down what I shared. As I strolled by, I asked if she would like to join me and my friends at our table. She immediately gathered her purse and belongings and followed me to the table.

As we sat down, I realized I hadn't actually introduced myself, and so we all exchanged introductions. She had come from Connecticut to get healing and to learn more about the prophetic. In a few moments, the Holy Spirit began to reveal more about my new friend. I told her that she was very happy during the day, but at night, she wanted to cry.

She looked me straight in the eyes and exclaimed, "Yes, I do, but I can't. I haven't cried in over twenty years." My heart broke as she revealed the pain of being unable to release all the pent-up emotions for so very long. She went on to say that she prayed that she would be healed at this conference, but her friend got healed instead. I looked at the elderly woman who had lost hope and asked one of the people with me for some tissues. I placed them in front of her.

I asked the woman if I could pray for her, and she nodded. Placing my hand on her shoulder, I began to pray in the spirit for my new friend. God began to show me her blockage was due to a fear of not knowing where her father was since his passing. Suddenly, I began weeping, answering all the questions she had for the Father about the whereabouts of her earthly dad. I began speaking for her as if I became her, repenting for what she blamed on her dad, forgiving him for what he did here on earth, releasing any and all judgments or accusations against him, and blessing him for being her father. I was sobbing as the words were all tumbling out as if a dam were released. Twenty years of bottled-up tears and fears were coming out like a tsunami, destroying any fear of the enemy that gripped her. When I was finished praying, she, too, was crying. Her healing had come just as she had prayed for, although it wasn't how she expected. She hugged and thanked me for my obedience. Her entire countenance had changed. She looked brighter, and her smile was even bigger than before.

When we follow the leading of the Holy Spirit, He will reveal all the hidden things about a person to set them free. This gifting includes words of knowledge: knowing something that is happening or has happened. God used those words of knowledge to open up the door of healing, setting her free of all that pain she was holding onto.

I didn't really understand the power we have in using the gifts of prophecy when ministering to individuals. We know what happened to the woman at the well when Jesus revealed everything about her. It changed her forever because she was free. No longer could her past keep her silent or hidden. She was released from shame, guilt, rejection, abandonment, and sin. Jesus waited for her to come, and this was a divine appointment to launch her into her destiny. So many times, we can get stuck, but God always has a plan to set us free. God realizes exactly what needs to be said in order to break those chains and open the door to freedom. I have received such unique words, images, and feelings while ministering with people. The one thing that doesn't surprise me is that whatever He tells me is always the truth.

Since being filled with the Holy Spirit in 2009, I have learned that God's Word will accomplish its task. God will move on those prophecies, whether quickly or if it takes years. The timing is always up to the Lord, and His timing is always perfect. Another truth I have learned is that our words are important as well. When we use God's Word in our prayers, they become words that agree with the truth and nature of God. The word or prophecy from the spirit allows you to move in both power and authority. God always has a plan; we simply need to release it into the atmosphere by speaking it into existence.

A short impression came to me; I wanted to buy hand mirrors as gifts for my Daddy's Girl Women's Conference. How wonderful to give such a practical and personalized gift to every woman attending. I began to research the cost, but it just wasn't feasible for this upcoming conference. We were in a pandemic with low registration. How could I justify this expense when that money could be put to better use? I put that idea on the back shelf for another time when life was not so crazy.

That same year, I went away for my birthday to the hills of Tennessee with a few close friends. The weather wasn't great one day, so we decided to stay in the cabin and watch the movie *Holy Ghost* by Darren Wilson. All of his movies document the moving of God through people. In one part of the movie, a pastor and his wife had a banquet for all the prostitutes in one of the cities of Thailand. They held this event after working hours so that no harm would come to the ladies. The pastors wanted to lavish love on these women. So they created goodie bags filled with makeup and other gifts that they gave out during dinner to bless each one. These ladies had such joy and excitement as they were opening these bags. What looked like a mirror was pulled out of the bag, and immediately, I thought of the vision God had given me about gifting hand mirrors.

Tears began to stream down my cheeks as this one scene from the movie was so personal. I got up from the sofa and went onto the deck of the house. As soon as I opened the door, the power of God fell on me. I cried out to Him, "I will get the mirrors. I don't care how much they cost. I will get them. I am so sorry for not being obedient and for allowing money to stop me from what you want to do."

The Lord said to me, "I will pay for them and for all your conferences." I burst into tears and began to praise Him for not only His goodness but His mercy. I gathered myself together and joined the rest of the ladies in the living room to finish watching the movie. As I sat there, a giddiness began to erupt inside me at the thought of purchasing the mirrors.

I came home and began to research the best place to order the mirrors. I found the perfect size, and the Lord gave me a verse to write on each mirror from Songs of Songs 4:7. "Every part of you is so beautiful, my darling. Perfect is your beauty."

The Lord said, "Each time they read this verse, they will know how I see them." I was so excited about what God was doing, and I shared this with a friend. She got excited, too, at how God was orchestrating it all. I told her that I knew that the Father was also going to provide the finances for the mirrors. She looked at me with such loving eyes and told me that she wanted to pay for them, and her husband would send me the money.

I was beyond speechless as my brain was still trying to process her words. I began to tear up and hugged her, asking if she was sure she wanted to do this. She chuckled and hugged me tighter. "We want to do this!" I thanked her and her husband and said my goodbyes.

That night, at home, I placed my order. Due to the pandemic, shipping was delayed, but I ordered early enough so it wouldn't be an issue. Or so I thought. I got one email saying that they would be late with a new delivery date. They called with the second notice, so I told them the final date that I needed the mirrors. The week they were supposed to be there, I got the notice they were in transit and should arrive on time.

The day before the conference, I had to pick up my speakers, Amie and Debbie, at the airport, run around for some last-minute items, and pack up the car for the event. I was so preoccupied that I did not realize the mirrors weren't there, and worse yet, I forgot about them.

The next day, we packed up the car, and the rest of the group met up at my house. I quickly checked the rooms to be sure I had packed everything for the weekend. I said goodbye to my family, kissed my dogs, and headed out the door. As soon as I opened the door, a vision of the mirrors appeared before me. The image immediately disappeared. They hadn't arrived the day before. After everything I went through to get them, I refused to leave without them.

I called the company to find out where they were, supposedly on a FedEx truck out for delivery. I asked what time they would arrive, but they couldn't give me an answer. I hung up and headed outside to tell my friends what was going on. "Okay, we need to pray!" We gathered in a circle and held hands. We needed those mirrors right then, and we were going to pray them in.

I started out the prayer, reminding God that these mirrors were for His daughters and that they were His idea in the first place. I reminded Him that I was obedient in ordering them and that they were detained due to the pandemic. I asked Him to dispatch angels to go and get that FedEx truck to my street. I thanked Him for hearing me and answering my prayers. Then this boldness came over me as I began to stomp my foot. "These mirrors *will* show up before we leave!"

I was putting a demand on heaven to move on my behalf. While I was stomping my foot, I declared I could hear the FedEx truck coming down my street even though no truck was in sight. I stomped my feet again and declared that the angels had rerouted that truck to my street; however, this time, I thought I heard the rumbling of a truck. It was so real, I opened my eyes to be sure that I was, in fact, hearing it, but again, no trucks were on my street. I declared louder, "Papa, I can hear the tires rolling toward my house, bringing me the mirrors." I began to shout.

Amie then shouted, "Wait, I hear them too!" I got so excited that we heard the same thing. We had prophesied the solution that I needed, so we finished praying in agreement. My friends appreciated my faith but were working on Plan B as to when we would have to leave for the conference. They all looked at me with weird smiles. They were trying to be excited and believe that our prayer would be answered, but just in case, they had me covered.

I was pulled away from the group by a phone call. "Lisa, God must really love you! The T-shirts you ordered had a major issue yesterday. The building lost all power. They called me last night to let me know the T-shirts would not be ready. I just got another phone call from the owner. The power went back on for a short time, and they were able to print your shirts before losing power again." I started to thank God for all His goodness when a loud rumbling came down the street. I quickly thanked my friend for handling the shirts and got off the phone right as the FedEx truck pulled up in front of my house. My friend was right. God really does love me!

We started shouting and praising God for His goodness yet again. The driver was confused by our celebration. We all cheered as he carried the box with the mirrors to my car. The ladies were taking pictures as this driver, unbeknownst to him, was part of the answer to a miracle prayer. We told him all about our prayer and then asked if we could pray and bless him. Gathering together, we thanked our heavenly Father for this driver and for answering our request. The driver said, "Amen" and told us we had made his day. We packed up and hit the road to see what Papa would do at the conference. To this day, Amie looks at the picture of that FedEx truck whenever she feels any doubt or disbelief about what God can do.

We discount the authority of ruling and reigning that God gave to Adam in the garden of Eden. Jesus came to give us back what was always supposed to be our right as His heirs. Many times, we accept what man says instead of what God says. We sing songs about ruling and reigning as children of God, yet we still don't get it. Life throws us a curve ball, and we simply duck, trying to avoid it, instead of swinging at it to knock it out of the ballpark. As children of God, we were created to be victors and not victims, to be overcomers against the adversities of life.

The Holy Spirit and the gifts we have been given are here to help us both war against the enemy and to fulfill the purpose the Father placed inside us. When we pray out those plans and stand in agreement with all He has purposed in our lives, we see God move miraculously.

Prophecy and Word of Knowledge:

Heavenly Father, I thank you that you have sent the Holy Spirit that lives and dwells inside me. I thank you, Holy Spirit, that you know all things. Just like Paul said, I ask you for the gift of prophecy so that I can exhort, encourage, and edify other believers. I thank you for words of knowledge that show you know everything about us. I ask you, Father, to activate these gifts of the Holy Spirit inside me. The Scriptures say you have not because you ask not, and so, I'm diligently asking. Holy Spirit, reveal to me the desires of the Father that will set others free. I thank you that every word of prophecy and word of knowledge is for the glory and honor of the Lord. Help me use these gifts to expand your kingdom. In Jesus's name, I pray. Amen.

CHAPTER 8

Worship and Praise

You can pass through his open gates with the password of praise. Come right into his presence with thanksgiving. Come bring your thank offering to him and affectionately bless his beautiful name!

Psalm 100:4

M an was created to worship and praise God because God is worthy of praise. In the Bible, worship and praise are so important. The book of Psalms has verse after verse that includes the words *worship* or *praise*. From Genesis to Revelation, worship and praise are on almost every page.

What is worship? Here is the definition of *worship* in *The Merriam-Webster Dictionary*: "1. to honor or show reverence for as a divine being or supernatural power 2. to regard with great or extravagant respect, honor, or devotion."[1]

The words in this description are powerful if we look at the biblical use. The word *honor* is mentioned 146 times in the Bible.[2] When we honor God, He honors us, and when we honor others, God rewards us with blessings. The word *reverence* means "deep respect for someone or something."[3] When we come to God, showing Him respect, we are acknowledging who He is. The last word is *devotion*. The definition is "deep love or loyalty."[4] Look at what Jesus told the disciples. "You shall love the Lord your God with all your heart, with all your soul, and with all your mind" (Mathew 22:37 NKJV). What Jesus was really saying was give God your *worship*.

The book of Psalms was originally called *Tehillim*, which means "praise songs" in Hebrew.[5] Although it was written by many authors, including Moses, King David wrote most of the Psalms. The Psalms were sometimes put to music to worship God, but all these poetic letters were written for God. This entire book was created for one thing: *worship*. Even today, you can read through the book of Psalms and find a situation that you might identify with. Reading the Psalms encourages you to praise God for who He is and what He has done. You will find a God who loves His people and who has always been faithful. In the Psalms, we see the importance of praise and worship when it comes to answered prayers.

Miriam's worship led the women of Israel into dancing and singing. God chose her as a prophet to teach and lead the people into worship. Miriam and her brother Moses wrote the first worship song in Exodus 15. "Then Miriam the prophetess, the sister of Aaron, took the timbrel in her hand; and all the women went out after her with timbrels and with dances. And Miriam answered them: 'Sing to the Lord, For He has triumphed gloriously! The horse and its rider He has thrown into the sea!'" (Exodus 15:20–21 NKJV). The worship and praise of the Israelites brought them victory as they conquered other nations and took back territory for God.

The pure worship of David carried the heart of God, and through that relationship, David became a king. He stripped himself of his kingly robes to dance and leap in a linen ephod before the Lord. His willingness to surrender everything, including his reputation, shows the great love he had for God. After having an affair with another man's wife, Bathsheba, David had that man killed and then married her. The prophet Nathan, sent by God, came to tell David that his son will die because of his sin. David bowed on the floor and fasted and prayed for seven days, but on the seventh day, his son died. David then got up, cleaned himself off, and went to the house of the Lord to worship. (See 2 Samuel 12.)

After Job received the news that all his children were dead, his servants were dead, and his flocks were taken or killed, Job went to worship and praise God. He didn't blame Him but acknowledged that every possession came from God and God could choose to take it all away. (See Job 1.)

Worship is a choice we make whenever we open our mouths. We can praise God for all He has done, or we can curse Him because things are not going the way we would like. In today's culture, we define worship as what the people on stage at church do when they sing. But worship is so much more than that.

In 2013, I received my first prophetic word from a well-known prophet, Jamie Galloway, at a Voice of the Prophet conference. This was only my second time in an environment where prophecy was flowing like a river. I was so excited to hear all the prophets and their encounters with God. Jamie Galloway was the first speaker of the day and was talking about seeing angels. As I leaned back in my seat and took it all in, the Father spoke to me. "Lisa, I am pulling you out from among the many and putting you in the spot-light." Panic filled me as my mind reeled with repentance for thinking such outlandish thoughts. I began apologizing to God for wanting to be recognized or thinking that I was special.

I shook my head, dismissed what I heard, and got excited again as Jamie Galloway took the stage and began to share all his stories of supernatural and angelic encounters. He held my attention as he talked about all the visible angelic activity around his home. I continued listening with such an excitement and began asking the Lord to have him pray over me so I would encounter angels too.

For the next two days, I continually prayed, asking for Jamie Galloway to pray over me. Oddly enough, everywhere I went, I saw him. God was putting me in his path at every turn, literally within touching distance of this man of God. My friend kept encouraging me to go up and ask him to pray over me. I said, "No way. I want God to do it. I only want it if God wants it for me."

The conference was everything I hoped for because I so wanted to understand my prophetic gifting and other gifts that the Holy Spirit gives us. We walked through the book area where every speaker had their books available with other recommended reading. One book by John Paul Jackson caught my eye: *I AM:365 Names of God*, a beautiful coffee-table book. I picked it up and said to my friend, Lisa, "I'm going to keep this book in my purse and have John Paul Jackson sign it on the elevator."

She laughed. "It fits in your bag perfectly." I purchased it and another book about dream interpretation.

After John Paul Jackson spoke at the morning session, I picked up my handbag and headed to our room to celebrate Lisa's birthday. I approached the elevator, and there was John Paul Jackson, waiting to get on. The doors opened, and we both stepped in. I asked him if he would sign my book and reached into my bag to pull it out. John Paul reached into his pocket for a pen. As he was writing, I nervously told him about a dream I had with him in it. I shared quickly what had happened in the dream, and then, without giving him a chance to speak, I told him what I thought it meant. He smiled, chuckled politely, and agreed with my interpretation. I thanked him for both signing my book and for all he taught me through his YouTube videos and special classes. The elevator stopped, and the doors opened. Turning back, I waved and thanked him again. I then realized that I had prophesied what just took place.

My friend, Lisa, finally got to the room and was so excited as she had a chance to talk with one of the speakers. She even got a prophetic word. *What a wonderful birthday gift,* I thought. We ate lunch and got ourselves together to go back down to the afternoon session. I went to refresh my makeup and wash my hands. I began thanking God for all He does and for blessing my friend on her birthday. He replied, "Don't be jealous. I have something for you too!" I was embarrassed, because I knew it was true. I apologized to God and headed back down to the conference.

Jamie Galloway was speaking again, so I sat down, eager to hear more of his stories. My friend, Lisa, was teasing me as Jamie was talking. I told her, "I just want to be prayed over by him."

Lisa said, "Do it, Lord, and take me with her!" We both chuckled for a few minutes and settled down to listen.

Jamie was beginning to tell a story when he paused for a few moments and shook his head. He looked down at the ground as if trying to pay attention to what he was hearing. Again, he started to speak, when he suddenly looked up. "I'm sorry, folks, but the Holy Spirit won't let this go, and I need to pray for a Lisa, actually Lisas." I took Lisa's hand, and we headed up to the front of the stage. Two other Lisas also came up to the stage.

I was the third Lisa to get prayer. I was surprised by what Jamie spoke over me because he told me I was a worshipper but not a worship leader or someone who sings on stage. Instead, he said I was a true worshipper of God. He continued that I had laid down something, but God was picking it back up. The only thing I had ever laid down in my life was my dream to become an actress. I was still trying to wrap my head around the fact that I was a worshipper.

As I mentioned earlier, I thought that being a worshipper and on stage was for the select few: those with the talents of singing or playing an instrument. All could worship, but not everyone was a worshipper. I loved singing and could get lost in worship for hours. I had some of my most incredible encounters during worship, yet I didn't understand the power we have in worship until Jesus showed me.

In January 2020, my sister called with the news that my father had suddenly passed. Shaking my head in disbelief, I asked, "What happened?" She told me he stood up and then collapsed. She tried to resuscitate him, but he was gone. My daddy had celebrated his eighty-eighth birthday two weeks earlier and seemed fine. The emotions began to hit as the shock wore off and reality was setting in. The tears began to fall as I slowly began processing my grief. I reached out to my siblings and relatives, retelling the news so my sister didn't have to do it. After all the calls were made, I sat in the quiet for a brief moment before I began to pray.

I asked the Lord, "Where is my daddy?" I suddenly saw my father sitting with Jesus, looking over a book. Jesus had His hand on my dad's shoulder, comforting him as he was turning the pages of this book with tears in his eyes.

God told me, "He is looking at his book.[6] His book was written in heaven about him. He is now seeing all the plans I had for him, and he saw the truth behind all the lies the enemy told him."

Seeing my dad cry was hard to watch, but Jesus wasn't condemning him for his choices. He was showing my daddy great love and compassion and how much He cared for him on earth, especially through the hard times. My dad was in heaven. He loved God so very much; the Lord once told me that my dad was like King David because of how my dad loved God. I laid on the couch, remembering all our conversations and thinking about the ones we would never have again. I thought about my childhood and how my dad changed when he found Jesus. My dad would go to church and worship; he loved worship most of all.

Later in the day, I again asked Jesus, "Where is my daddy?"

Jesus quickly responded that he was seeing heaven. I asked, "Can I see him?"

He responded, *"No."* Holding back tears of disappointment, I accepted the fact that God had already shown me my father and God was with him. I apologized for asking and said I would not ask again. I told Jesus how I wish I would have gone to Florida earlier to see my dad. The guilt of postponing my visits to Florida meant I would not get one last hug from Daddy. That was a hard pill to swallow. I made the decision the night before that I would book a flight to see my parents, only to get the call the next morning that I was too late.

The woulda, coulda, shoulda thoughts raced through my mind as despair gripped my heart tighter and tighter. The enemy was using every memory and decision I made against me to keep me in shame and condemnation.

I was trying to pull myself together so I could actually do something without crying. I felt as if I were caught in an ocean riptide. I could see myself getting out of the storm of grief, but then a dark hand would grab my ankle and pull me back in. This was not simply grief but something more that wanted a hold of me. I tossed and turned all night long as the storm raged inside me.

I woke up the next morning and made plans to go to Florida to be with my mom and siblings. As soon as my foot hit the floor, the wave of guilt smacked me in the face. I couldn't think or eat, and I could care less how I looked. I went to work to see if I could get my thoughts together but wound up leaving after a few hours. I called my husband and told him I was going to my friend Lori's, because she was having a guest speaker at her Friday night church gathering. I told him I needed to go; I needed to worship the Lord.

I arrived at Lori's house and fell into her arms as she opened the door. She held me and comforted me until I was ready to move. I was right where I was supposed to be. The rest of her guests came in and hugged me. Some knew what had happened, and some were finding out as they arrived. I wasn't my usual chatty self as people were milling about and eating. Looking at the food made me sick, and watching everyone's joy was painful. I found a seat in the back and planted myself there until worship started.

I struggled to hold back the tears and stay composed. The atmosphere began to shift as the worship started. Usually at these events, I could quickly engage with heaven and encounter the Father but not this time. I told Jesus, "I don't want anything. I just want to worship you." The music began to swell as the hearts of those attending joined in the celebration of love for our heavenly Papa.

Malik Edwards was speaking and leading everyone into the heavenly realms with his worship and praise. He shouted, "Everyone stand up, and let's worship our *King!*" I stood in obedience to what the Holy Spirit wanted. I put my hands out in front of me with my palms open toward heaven as if I were waiting for a gift.

I was sobbing uncontrollably as my head hung low, covering the grief that so firmly gripped my heart. I was singing along although I felt completely disconnected. My hair was now sticking to my wet face, and I couldn't even bother to brush it out of my eyes. My eyes were closed as I sang, the words broken up by chokes of sorrow and deep breaths to control my emotions.

I shook my head and thought, *Nothing is going to stop me from worshipping God.* Suddenly, I saw a vision. My hands were out in front of me. I saw my shoulders and then the top of my head. A golden mist was rising off my body as if steam were rising off a hot pavement after a brief rain shower. The mist was increasing as it floated up. This was not from my perspective but from a heavenly one.

Above me, looking down through an open portal was Jesus, and standing next to Him was my earthly daddy. Jesus had His arm around my dad as He was showing him something new. There was a large opening with a gate or a bar that encircled the portal but a set boundary would not allow you to go too far although you could see. I was allowed to witness this beautiful moment between a father and a son. Jesus pulled my dad closer to Him as they watched me. The golden mist was now filling the portal as Jesus begun speaking to my dad. "Bill," he said, "look at your daughter worshipping me. Through her sorrow, through her tears, she is worshipping me. She is choosing to worship me."

Jesus then leaned over this portal in heaven and took a deep breath, pulling the golden mist into his nostrils. He withdrew from the portal and spoke to my dad again. "Smell that, Bill. That's pure worship." He turned and looked into my dad's eyes. "She learned that from you, and because of that, you will be rewarded up here for everything she does on earth!"

In a blink of an eye, I was inside the portal in heaven, and my daddy's arms embraced me in the biggest hug ever. I couldn't see him, yet I could hear him. He held me tightly as he whispered how much he loved me, how he was so proud of me, and that he read my book in heaven. He kissed me on my forehead and told me that he was praying for me. In an instant, I was back in worship at my friend's.

The tears still streaming down my face changed from sorrow to complete joy. I knelt down and thanked the Lord for allowing such a healing to my heart. The grief lifted off as if it were a blanket that I no longer needed. I excused myself from my seat and headed to the kitchen. Lori followed me to see if I was okay. I hugged her as I began unpacking what I just saw in the spirit and excitedly shared every detail. My emptiness was replaced by the knowledge that both my heavenly and earthly fathers were watching me from above.

I finally understood the importance of worship and why both David and Job chose to worship in their grief. In the worship, we feel connected from the broken places in our lives. The heart of worship through grief is the sweet offering we can give to God. Choosing to give what little we have is considered the best offering. According to Jesus, "For the rich only gave out of their surplus, but she sacrificed out of her poverty and gave to God all that she had to live on, which was everything she had" (Mark 12:44). Jesus was referring to the widow who only had two coins left in her pocket, yet she gave all she had. Worship is easy when life is good, but when everything around you is crashing down, can you still worship?

David worshipped after his son died, and Job worshipped when all his children had died and when everything was taken from him. This pure worship—in brokenness, pain, loss, suffering, anguish, betrayal, rejection, abandonment, hurt, and despair—removes the performance part of celebrating God. The fragrant smell written in the book of Songs of Songs says, "How satisfying to me, my equal, my bride. Your love is my finest wine—intoxicating and thrilling. And your sweet, perfumed praises—so exotic, so pleasing" (Song of Songs 4:10). We release this in the purest praise from our hearts. Throughout Psalm 66, we can see that worship and fragrance are offered as a sacrifice of our love to God.

Amazingly enough, all creation was created to worship; however, we are still given the choice of who we will worship. Worship is the currency of heaven, and God recognizes its rewards. In my vision, Jesus told my dad that he would be rewarded for my worship and praise here on earth. Worship is more than singing songs but is an offering of ourselves as a living sacrifice to advance the kingdom. We worship Him in spirit and in truth. These keys unlock heaven and release a move of God.

I was attending a conference where one of the speakers, apostle Anthony Turner, had to stay in his room during the evening session. He was in extreme pain and couldn't stand or put any pressure on his feet due to gout. His wife, Alicia, shared about his symptoms. I began to immediately pray in the spirit and intercede for his healing. I sensed I needed to pray over him although I didn't know him. I had heard of him and that he was an incredible worshipper. Mutual friends mentioned him to me (and vice versa) in different conversations, so we were both excited to finally meet. After the morning session, he rode his scooter over to me. He pulled up with a huge smile, almost as if he already knew me. "Lisa Perna, we finally meet!"

I smiled back. "Anthony Turner, I have heard a great deal about you too. I am so happy to finally meet you as well. But before I get to know you, can I pray over you?"

Anthony nodded. "Yes, please do." I asked him if he wanted to do it then or later, because everyone was leaving for lunch. He said, "No, let's do it now."

As soon he gave his permission, I couldn't even look at him and turned my face away because the presence of the Lord was so strong. I began breathing out as the heaviness was so thick that I had to blow out the weightiness. Slowly, the heaviness brought me to my knees to touch his feet. My hand was turning into the instrument that the Holy Spirit would use to love on His son.

I began praying in my spiritual language as the Holy Spirit shared the secrets of the Father and His desire to heal Anthony. A great love began filling my heart for this man that I had just met. I began to weep as I continued praying for Anthony and all the pain he was in. This love so overwhelmed me that I now viewed him in a totally new way. No longer was he a stranger, but through the Holy Spirit, he was being knit into my heart. I looked up at him, and through tears, I told him how much God loved him and how so many people, including his wife, Alicia, had been contending for his healing.

As this beautiful wife prayed for her husband, I could not speak as the tears represented all the love being poured out and filling the cup in heaven with intercession for him. He looked down at me with gratitude as slight physical changes started to happen, and the heat increased in his leg. I started to speak to gout and command it to leave. My declarations grew bolder as I now began contending for the healing of my new friend who was being positioned by God as a spiritual father.

In this supernatural moment, we both became aware that we would develop a long-term relationship. I finished praying and asked Anthony how he was feeling. He smiled and said the pain had lessened. Quickly I stood and asked him to do the same.

I took his hand, and he stood from the scooter. He looked at me. "I couldn't stand at all this morning."

Smiling, I said, "Okay, on a scale from one to ten, where is your pain now?"

He said he was at a seven, but that morning, he was at a twelve. He chuckled.

I winked at him. "Let's get this down to a six. Are you ready?" I grabbed his hand. "Let's walk."

As we took our first step of faith together hand in hand, I started to remind God of who He is and all the promises He has given to us. I called on His name, the great healer Jehovah Rapha, on behalf of his son Anthony. I said, "You are the Great Physician and our Healer. In the Bible, Lord, you gave Moses a bronze serpent on a pole to heal the children of Israel, and if they looked at it, they were healed. You gave us an even greater promise of healing as Your Son Jesus hung on a tree for all our sickness and diseases. The Scriptures say that Jesus was broken and bruised for all our iniquities, and by His stripes, we are healed.[7] I didn't say this, Lord. You said it in your Word and through your prophets. I am calling you to perform all that you have promised." After I stopped, I turned to Anthony and again asked him, "What is your pain level?"

He smiled. "It's a six!"

Now we were both excited as I said, "Let's go to a five." I immediately saw Anthony singing in a vision, and I asked him if he could sing a song. We were going to worship to a pain level of five. I had forgotten that Anthony was a worship leader and his songs change atmospheres. While you are in the spirit, you sometimes forget what you actually know. Anthony began singing as we continued to walk, holding hands as the worship filled the room. The joy was overwhelming as his song echoed in the now empty room. He was singing this melody of adoration that declared the goodness of God. This childlike feeling overtook us as we started swinging our hands back and forth like a father with his child.

Anthony stopped singing, and I asked him again, "Where is your pain now?"

He turned, smiled, and said, "It's a five!" Laughter took over as we were swinging our hands and singing how good our Papa was.

I said, "Let's go to DEFCON 4," and we both began laughing, overflowing with joy and getting drunk in the Spirit. We both started to thank God, because we knew that this was a done deal. I declared his healing was completed and continued thanking God for all His goodness. I turned once again. "Well?"

Anthony said, "It's a two and a half." With that, I started jumping up and down in glee as we were both witnessing this miracle taking place.

I shouted, "DEFCON 1, here we come!" In one last vision, we were not moving, simply resting in the truth that this was finished.

I stopped walking and told Anthony we just need to be still and know He is God. In my spirit, a song was being sung about rest, and I asked Anthony to once again sing about rest. Soon, the room was filled with a peace that took away any doubt that he would not be completely healed. Anthony stopped singing and turned to me. "It's a one!"

I hugged him. "I have one more thing to ask you." I turned to pick up my belongings. "You can drive over to lunch on your scooter or walk with me. I don't want to pressure you, and it is a long walk."

Anthony once again smiled. "I will walk with you." My heart leaped as we were going to see this through together.

Hand in hand, we started walking to the building where lunch was being served. Our conversation was filled with the excitement of not only this miraculous healing but how we both felt about our new friendship. I shared the visions I had, and he shared how he felt as I was praying for him as if I were his daughter, contending for his healing. I told him that was how I was praying. We knew that yes, indeed, we were meant to meet and partner together for future projects.

As we arrived at the building, I opened the door for Papa T, as I now affectionately called him, and let go of his hand. He walked in by himself to the welcome of cheering. Everyone was overjoyed as he was not only standing but walking with no signs of pain. I joined in the celebration of both a miracle and a divine connection appointed in heaven.

Worship and Praise:

Heavenly Father, you are worthy to be praised. Let my lips speak of your goodness and your faithfulness all the days of my life. Let everything that I do be an act of worship to you. I surrender all of me to worship all of you. I thank you, Lord, that our hearts are intertwined as I worship you. I thank you, Holy Spirit, that my mouth exalts the words that cannot even express the love that I have. Jesus, you said that if we don't worship, the rocks will cry out. Help me be the vessel that shouts from the top of the mountain that you are Lord. Let my very breath bring a sweet offering of praise to your ears, let my every move become a sweet fragrance to your nose, and let my heart continually sing of your worthiness. Take my eyes off others and keep them fixed on you as I go through my day, worshipping you and all that you have done. Let my very life be the greatest worship to you, my King. In Jesus's name. Amen.

CHAPTER 9

Praying in Tongues and Seeing in the Spirit

So here's what I've concluded. I will pray in the Spirit, but I will also pray with my mind engaged. I will sing rapturous praises in the Spirit, but I will also sing with my mind engaged.
~ 1 Corinthians 14:15

R ight before Jesus ascended into heaven, He told the disciples to tarry or wait in Jerusalem to receive power from on high. The people would be gathered there for the celebration of Shavuot, which meant "latter firstfruits". This festival was fifty days after Passover, and the Israelites celebrated the day that God gave Moses the law (the Ten Commandments). Jesus prophesied to the disciples that they would be empowered with the Holy Spirit.

Since the day that Moses brought down the law or the Torah from Mount Sinai, the consequence of not following it has been death. The first set of the Ten Commandments written by the finger of God in stone was destroyed by the hands of Moses. As a result of his anger against the Israelites because of their disobedience, three thousand men died. Moses had to go back up Mount Sinai in order to get another copy of the Ten Commandments, although this time, the law would be written by the hand of Moses and not the finger of God. (See Exodus 34.)

The disciples knew the law, and yet they met grace when Jesus entered their lives. They now saw the law in a new way: through the eyes of love as their perspective flipped from death to abundant life. They watched Jesus walk in power and authority, and they marveled that they could do the same by speaking His name.

They waited with eager anticipation for the coming of the Holy Spirit. They remembered what Jesus told them before He ascended back to heaven. "Jesus instructed them, 'Don't leave Jerusalem, but wait here until you receive the gift I told you about, the gift the Father has promised. For John baptized you in water, but in a few days from now you will be baptized in the Holy Spirit!'" (Acts 1:4–5). Jesus further told the disciples, "But I promise you this—the Holy Spirit will come upon you, and you will be seized with power. You will be my messengers to Jerusalem, throughout Judea, the distant provinces —even to the remotest places on earth!" (Acts 1:8).

The upper room was filled with 120 people, including the disciples of Jesus, when a mighty rushing wind came down from heaven. "They were all filled and equipped with the Holy Spirit and were inspired to speak in tongues—empowered by the Spirit to speak in languages they had never learned! "(Acts 2:4). It was just as Jesus had promised. The Holy Spirit moved over the room in power. They all began to speak in a new language as the fire of God filled them with this new living water. According to *Strong's Concordance*, the Greek word for "tongues" is *glossa*, which means "of uncertain affinity; the tongue; by implication a language (specifically one naturally unacquired)."[1]

God is a God of restoration, and He always finds a way to give back what has been taken away or stolen. At one point, all the people on earth spoke the same language and worked together in unity. These descendants of Noah gathered themselves to build a high tower that reached to the heavens. When God saw what they were doing, He went down to investigate further. "But the Lord came down to see the city and the tower which the sons of men had built. And the Lord said, 'Indeed the people are one and they all have one language, and this is what they begin to do; now nothing that they propose to do will be withheld from them'" (Genesis 11:5–6 NKJV).

God was concerned that man would be able to take over the world with unrighteous motives, and so He had a plan to stop what they were doing. "'Come, let Us go down and there confuse their language, that they may not understand one another's speech.' So, the Lord scattered them abroad from there over the face of all the earth, and they ceased building the city" (Genesis 11:7–8 NKJV). The heart of the Father is unity with one another, but He also wants us to have righteous and pure motives.

In Acts 1:13–14, they were all working in one accord, praying in full agreement. The Passion Translation says, "gripped with one passion, interceding and waiting in prayer." They all had the right hearts for God to restore one language that would declare the truths of His kingdom. The reason for tongues or a spiritual language was a restoration of what was lost at the Tower of Babel. God could now convey His thoughts, desires, and plans through man, who was given back the authority through His Son, Jesus.

In addition to the restoration of the Tower of Babel, redemption even restored the three thousand who were killed in Exodus when Peter gave the people the choice to follow God. "Peter preached to them and warned them with these words: 'Be rescued from the wayward and perverse culture of this world!' Those who believed the word that day numbered three thousand. They were all baptized and added to the church" (Acts 2:40–41).

From the moment I received my prayer language, everything changed. A whole new world opened up for me. I began to both speak in a spiritual way and also see in the spiritual realm. This new way of communicating with the Father was enlightening and exciting. I was enrolled in Holy Spirit University, where you didn't get a diploma but received a new level of understanding.

Speaking or praying in tongues is your spirit coming into agreement with the perfect will of God. Some believers don't like or even believe in tongues, because they don't know what they are praying and can't understand themselves. The Holy Spirit completely takes control; He knows exactly how to pray and intercede. As I stated earlier, I knew about the benefits of tongues or praying in the spirit because of my dad. After receiving the baptism of the Holy Spirit and my spiritual language, I enjoyed praying all the more in the spirit and found myself doing it constantly.

No one told me how often to pray in the spirit, but the apostle Paul encouraged this practice many times in the New Testament. He wrote in Ephesians 6 that as part of our spiritual armor, we should pray in the spirit at all times. Praying in the spirit increases or builds up our spirit man. I prayed in the spirit because I loved feeling so close to God. It was my very own secret language that no one else could understand.

I spent hours in prayer as soon as my kids got on the school bus. As I said earlier, Facebook was filled with prayer requests as I scrolled through my feed every day. I was told to scroll past certain prayer requests and stop on others I normally would have passed by. My spirit began praying as the Holy Spirit dropped faces into my mind of people that I knew. As each face popped into my head, the prayer of intercession burst forth as prompted by the Holy Spirit.

I cried and rocked as I addressed the petitions of those names to God. I didn't understand that I was being used as an intercessor; I thought this was how everyone prayed. Not only was my spirit engaged, but my mind was too. God was training me to be sensitive to His Spirit by praying for people that I didn't know. The Father would share secrets as I prayed in tongues. He then revealed His heart for one of His children.

After a full year of time with the Father, I was brought back into the marketplace. I had been a stay-at-home mom for the past twelve years. Our finances had taken a hit, and we needed insurance for the family. I prayed one morning and saw a Craigslist logo in a vision. The Lord said, "Go there." I Googled "Craigslist" and looked into job openings. There was an open position in cosmetics at a department store at a nearby mall. I had worked in cosmetics before having children and swore I would never go back, but here, God was sending me back.

I applied for the part-time position, which was perfect until a full-time job opened up. It wouldn't take long before I would begin revealing both the outer and the inner beauty of the women who came to my counter. Since I already had a routine of praying in tongues as I cleaned my home, taking the Holy Spirit to work seemed natural. I now prayed in tongues as I cleaned the counter or restocked shelves. The mundane tasks at work became my happy place as I got to spend time with God.

The Holy Spirit soon began to change the atmosphere around my makeup counter. The ladies who worked with me began to notice something was happening in the cosmetic department. There was joy and peace, and the worries of the world seemed to melt away. Soon, the ladies from other counters began asking questions about God. Sales at my counter had doubled since my arrival. God was clearly moving in and around me.

I didn't really understand all the supernatural stuff or everything to do with the Holy Spirit, so I kind of went with the flow. One lady came to my counter, looking for mascara for her daughter. We casually chatted, and soon the conversation turned to God. He always had a funny way of doing that. She asked me what church I was attending and shared the church where she was a leader. My husband knew her pastor, so we continued chatting as I was ringing up her items. She looked at me, smiled, and then said, "You know you are a seer, right?" I shook my head and then asked if there was anything else that she saw in me. Again, with a smile and a wink, she told me I was an intercessor.

I thanked her for her kind words and handed her the items she purchased. I had no idea what any of those words meant, but she spoke as if they were important.

I called one of my friends who was more spiritually in tune than me and shared the recent encounter. "So, can you tell me what a seer is?"

She said, "Oh, that is not a good thing. The Bible clearly tells us to beware of seers and soothsayers."

I shook my head at her words. "No, I think you might be wrong. This lady seemed kind of excited about it. Also, do you know what an intercessor is?"

A long pause followed with a quick answer. "Nope, I've never heard that word before."

I hung up the phone and wondered about this friend's response. This gave me the nudge to do some further research.

The next day, my friends and I drove over to the Jesus Gift and Book Store in a nearby town. I began to search the rows of books, looking for one on intercessors. So many books were written about faith, spiritual warfare, and many other topics, but I couldn't find anything on intercessors. After looking through the entire store, I went to ask the person at the register for some help. The manager came out and walked me over to a section of books I thought I had already looked at. She said, "There they are," and she pointed out four books.

Jokingly, I said, "Wow, such a large selection to choose from." *The Happy Intercessor* by the late Beni Johnson caught my eye.

I thought, *Well, if I am called to be an intercessor, I might as well be a happy one.* I chuckled to myself. God has a great way of answering your questions and putting everything into proper perspective.

To this day, *The Happy Intercessor* is one of my favorite books. It taught me about prayer and the role God has for the intercessors who truly are the watchmen on the wall. We are all called to pray, but God uses the intercessors to pray for specific assignments. This book also addressed the truth about being a seer, which was exactly who I am, a person who sees what God is showing them in the spirit. Beni Johnson's teachings helped me understand God's call on my life. God then showed me how to walk into that calling.

After reading that book, something opened up in and around me, because my cosmetic counter turned into a place of ministry. First, my colleagues asked me to pray over them. They were skeptical at first, because some had been hurt by well-meaning Christians who wanted to beat Jesus into them rather than introducing them to Him. One of the ladies from another counter was of Jewish descent. She made it clear that she was very proud of her Hebraic roots and had no intentions of changing.

God had given me such a love for the Jewish culture and the Old Testament. I talked to my friend about the Torah and the stories in the Bible. She asked me questions about my relationship with God and watched as I ministered to others. I laughed when she told me she would come to my church if I had one, but she would remain Jewish.

Spending time in prayer for people opens up an opportunity for God to move in ways that will forever impact them. Jesus showed the heart of the Father by building relationships. God was instructing me to do the same thing as every conversation about Him was ministering to the listener. The deeper a person begins to trust you, the deeper you are allowed to go. Now I knew that my Jewish friend had some serious fear issues, but one day, these manifested in front of me. She broke down as she began talking about bed bugs and how she thought she had accidentally been near someone who had been in an establishment that had an outbreak. She was sobbing uncontrollably, and at that point, I confronted this demonic stronghold of fear and kicked it to the curb.

I ran over to her counter and wrapped my arms around my hysterical friend. I told her that she didn't have to live like this any longer. It was time to break free from the grip of fear. In tears, she nodded, and we went outside the store to a spot that I called my office. I grabbed her hands and told her that we were going to invite Jesus and the Holy Spirit to come. Once again, she nodded. I began to pray in tongues and asked if I could put my hand on her heart. The stronghold of fear began lifting as it encountered the perfect love that was flowing into my friend.

The words began to fall as I commanded the grip of fear to leave her. My eyes were closed, but I knew she was crying although not a sound was coming from her. I tightened my grip on her hands and told her she needed to repent and come out of agreement with fear. God was so much bigger, but she believed that fear was bigger than Jesus. She agreed and began to repent and ask for forgiveness for believing all the lies that fear told her.

Suddenly, I felt as if we were pulled up into a whirlwind that spun wildly around us, stripping off anything that was not of God. A tornado of His love encircled us, lifting us into a new stratosphere of freedom.

As I finished praying with my eyes still closed, we came back to the ground. As soon as we touched down, I opened my eyes. My friend was smiling with tears of joy that replaced the cries of fear. I told her what I thought was my imagination. To my surprise, she had experienced the same thing. She felt as if she were floating in the air with a whirlwind swirling around her. We hugged, and she thanked me. I winked. "Don't thank me, thank Jesus."

She sheepishly lowered her eyes. "Thank you, Jesus."

You never really know how prayer affects a person until you see the change in them. A few days later, my friend came into work with the biggest smile I had ever seen. She ran over and hugged me. "Guess what, I went to a store and tried on clothes for the first time in three years. I didn't even think or worry once about those bedbugs! Fear was kicked to the curb, thanks to Jesus!"

I giggled. "Yes, it was!"

My little cosmetic counter became a place of encounters with God as I walked around, praying in the spirit. The Lord prepared the atmosphere, releasing the presence of God for all. This was a very special time in my life. God was teaching me how to care for and love His daughters. David was first called to be a shepherd, but he had a greater calling to be a king. He had to learn how to tend and care for the sheep before he could be trusted to rule over Israel. The same thing was happening to me. Although I am not called to be a king, God had a greater purpose for me to walk in.

I learned so much during the four-and-one-half years I worked in cosmetics. The greatest lesson was how much God loved His daughters. God revealed His goodness as each lady came for her appointment with the King. I prayed quietly in the spirit as He spoke the truth about each daughter He sent. I quickly knew if this was an assignment from the heavenlies or just someone coming in to purchase a new lipstick. My husband joked, "Lipstick or prayer? Oh, prayer Lisa will be in soon," whenever I told him about my latest encounter.

The store managers soon heard about the miracles and healings that took place at the cosmetic counter. I never tried to push my beliefs about Jesus on anyone or change their religion. The Father had opened up a portal to release His love, and I was just the conduit, showing His love through signs, wonders, and miracles, as Jesus instructed. Some of the employees had heard about me and came by on their breaks to chat or sat with me at lunch to hear about God and His Son, Jesus.

Through the relationships that I built, some reached out beyond work to their family and friends. Soon, I was ministering outside the store and in people's homes. People formed trust not only with me but with the Jesus living inside me. I was praying for and receiving texts from my co-workers' family members, asking for prayer as well.

I got a frantic text from Maria, one of my co-workers. Please call me. I clicked on the phone icon on my cell, and she answered in tears. I barely got a hello out when she said that her nine-year-old nephew Cristian was in the hospital and they were not sure what was wrong. I told her I would start praying and to please text me when she learned more. She fearfully told me that they thought he might have cancer. I tried to reassure her that it would be okay and told her not to come into agreement with anything she heard.

I hung up the phone and went into full-on warfare prayer. The Holy Spirit bubbled up with cries and groans that were not mine but my friend's. As I was praying, I received another text, this time, from Cristian's mother.

The Dr. at the hospital has diagnosed him with cancer. He has a lump in his kidneys and white mass around his chest. They think it's leukemia, please pray.

I texted his mom back, telling her I was on it. Maria then texted me again, repeating what her sister had just shared. Fear was gripping these sisters at the news of the doctors' diagnosis.

Putting down my phone, I closed my eyes, allowing my spirit to enter the throne room of God. Hebrews 4:16 says that we are to go boldly to the throne room, and there we will receive mercy and find grace. We do not enter as slaves but as sons and daughters going to talk with our heavenly Father. I was not going for my request but for a friend who didn't know how to engage in spiritual conversation. In words my human mind could not comprehend, my prayers continued pouring out a petition throughout the day for healing. I prayed for a turnaround in the hospital for this young boy. I spoke to all the issues he was facing and told his body to get back into perfect order.

Six hours later, Jennifer texted again, saying that Cristian was doing better, and his oxygen was rising. Thank you, your prayers are working.

I continued praying in the spirit the rest of the day. As soon as I woke up the next day, I texted Maria and asked her how Cristian was doing. As I drank a cup of coffee and waited for a response, I went to my place of prayer. As I curled up and thanked God for His goodness, my cell dinged with a report from Jennifer on all the protocols they would have to perform on her son. The doctors had drained the fluids from his lung, which helped him breathe, and the tumor had shrunk a bit. They had started chemo and steroids. When they checked Cristian's blood, the cancer levels had gone down.

I became angry at the injustice of children becoming sick and getting cancer. Putting my coffee down, I began to have a real conversation with the Father. Asking God the hard questions about life and challenging the ways of the world is not always fun. You never know how He will answer, and some answers may surprise you. I picked up my coffee and took another sip as I awaited His response. My prayer language bubbled up as tears slowly rolled down my cheeks. The Father clearly told me that Cristian would be healed and that he would live.

I was so excited after hearing that this situation was about to be turned around that I texted Maria. I told her that we simply needed to stand in agreement that Cristian would be healed. Jennifer was keeping me updated on Cristian's progress. I replied that she should start speaking to the cancer and tell it to shrivel up and die in Jesus's name. This was spiritual warfare 101, and I was teaching her how to fight for her baby. Every problem that her son was having, I had her pray the opposite. Her son began responding to his mother's prayers and declarations.

After seven days, Cristian was still in the hospital and still not 100 percent back to normal. His mom was texting me with each improvement and what issues he was still having. In prayer, the Holy Spirit gave me strategies, and I shared them with Jennifer. I continued to pray all through the day in my heavenly language as I felt breakthrough was coming.

The next day, I got the news that we were all praying for: The tumor was gone! After only eight days, Cristian was doing so much better that they were getting ready to release him. Jennifer was so excited that the tumor and disappeared, *and* the cancer they called cell blasts in his blood was gone too. The doctors were so surprised there was no trace of cancer after only eight days.

The doctors treating Cristian felt that the cancer might return due to its aggressive nature. So they recommended a protocol of a heavy treatment of chemo for a year with a reassessment after completion. As soon as I heard this, I became angry and felt as if these doctors refused to believe that Cristian was completely healed. His mom tried to figure out another treatment possibility but was strongly encouraged by the doctor to proceed with chemo.

My anger increased, and my mercy kicked in at the same time. I cried that this was being forced, and so I prayed for protection over Cristian as he went through all his treatments.

Periodically, Jennifer messaged me about how Cristian's progress. For the most part, he was doing well and seemed to be handling the chemo. But seven months later, I got a message that Cristian had an infection in his rectum that caused pneumonia in his lungs. He was in the ICU on a ventilator and receiving antibiotics to help clear the infection. I told her I would begin to pray.

My morning assignment of prayer for Cristian for the next few days was fueled by Jesus and coffee. I prayed in the spirit about what was going on in the natural and in the spiritual. As I messaged back and forth with Jennifer, she told me I was on the right track. As I prayed, his condition began to improve. With each new revelation, I told her how to pray over her son. She was praying and fighting for him with everything she had.

Disclaimer: Some of the upcoming content may be graphic, but I wanted to stay true to the vision as I saw it.

On the ninth morning, I poured my coffee and began to pray for Cristian, but something was different. I was taken into an open vision where I saw a small anus with a yellow puss-filled sore toward the bottom. This image appeared right in my face, probably not the first thing you want to see in the morning before drinking coffee. Just then, Jennifer texted me and said that he had this bad infection that was making him very sick on his bottom. Due to the chemo, his body was too weak to fight. She went on to say that they were going to give him a colostomy bag so that when he woke up, he didn't make it worse by having a bowel movement. Her fear and frustration came through each of her texts. God was showing me what needed to be healed first in this vision.

I asked her if the sore was on his anus and described what I had just seen. She responded that I had seen correctly. I began praying as I could still see this vision. The infection was highlighted to me, and using my finger in midair, I began to clear it out. My fingernail began breaking up and flicking away the yellow pieces of bacteria. The wound was actually very deep, and I was digging deeper until all the yellow was gone. The raw skin under the infection was irritated. The Lord then said to blow on the skin. I started to blow into the vision before me, and much to my surprise, the skin began to visibly heal. Again, I blew into the image before me, and the next layer of skin was healed. The more I blew on the wound, the more the deepest layers seemed to heal.

As soon as I finished, the image disappeared. I sat in shock for a few minutes, trying to understand my vision. I texted Jennifer to share what had just happened without sounding too weird. God knew what needed to be done, and He simply needed someone to partner with Him. Six hours later, I got another text from Jennifer. The nurse had come in to clean the wound and said it looked better than it did the day before.

The next day, the doctors assessed the wound, cleaned it, and determined it was healing. They canceled the colostomy bag procedure. His kidneys began producing enough urine, so they took him off dialysis. Three days later, they took him off a ventilator; eighteen days later, he was moved out of ICU; and fifty-seven days later, he was finally sent home. As I write this in 2022, Cristian is now a freshman in high school. His story constantly reminds me that God will fulfill His promises.

Many times, during the course of his healing, it didn't look good and even seemed like he was losing the battle. During the entire time I prayed for him, the Spirit of God said to declare, stand, and fight. I believed he would be healed, and I am so happy to report that he is cancer free.

We don't always understand what we see in the spirit realm. The mind will tell us that this is only our imagination, religion will tell us that it's the devil, but that soft whisper from our spirit will tell us it's God. I have seen many body parts in my spirit, later to find out that what I saw was real. The Holy Spirit has revealed medical terms that I never heard before to show me that God really knows all things. Learning to trust that God speaks to me in visions has helped me pray for people. It is a game changer as I know that I'm speaking the will of God when I'm praying through the Holy Spirit. We are all called to heal the sick, just like Jesus. The Messiah saw what needed to be done, and He spoke what needed to be said. He changed the world one person or miracle at a time, and we need to do the same.

Praying in Tongues and Seeing in the Spirit:

Heavenly Father, thank you for the Holy Spirit. Thank you that as I open my mouth, He fills it with words too heavenly to understand. Help me wield my sword of the Spirit, praying in the spirit at all times. I ask you to give me endurance to pray passionately, continually interceding in all manner of prayer. Holy Spirit, I ask you to give me eyes to see. Remove the scales that are blocking my vision in the spiritual realms. Help me encounter you with my words and my vision. Help me say what you want to be said and help me see what you show me. I thank you, Lord, for opening up my spiritual senses. Help me stay attentive to your whispers and the glimmers that you reveal through the Holy Spirit. I thank you that in the same way Jesus saw what you did, so shall I see. I thank you in Jesus's name. Amen.

CHAPTER 10
Repentance and Forgiveness

Fools mock the need for repentance,
while the favor of God rests upon all his lovers.
~ Proverbs 14:9

I n the three years of Jesus's ministry, He healed the sick, cast out demons, and raised the dead. Many Scriptures show how some individuals were healed, and after the healing, Jesus forgave them of their sin. In fact, He told them to go and sin no more. Not only did He forgive them, but He told them not to do it again. How many times do we ask for forgiveness only to do it again?

The word "repentance" in Greek is *metanoeo* and means "change of mind, thought, or thinking so powerful that it changes one's very way of life."[1] In other words, it means a complete turnaround from how you previously lived. When we become born-again believers in Jesus Christ, we should live completely differently than we did before we knew Him. As we look at the lives of those in the New Testament, we can see the difference from before Jesus to after Jesus.

God gave Moses the law to keep the Israelites from sinning, but that was not enough. The sinful nature arose even after God had taken them out of Egypt. The Lord gave them the wealth of Egypt, but they used that wealth to build a golden calf to worship. This broke the first law of the commandments, and death was the penalty. Moses invited all who wanted to stand with God to come and stand by him. After the Israelites chose their side, Moses then ordered those who were standing next to him to go and kill those who were not. In all, three thousand were killed.

Moses told the tribes of Israel about even more rules and parameters established by God. His heart was that they would stay clear of sin, but they still continued breaking the law. The sacrifice of animals and their blood kept the judgment of the Lord away for only a short time. God had a better plan, one that He had prepared before the foundations of time. Sin blocked the way to fellowship between God and man. The only blood that would cover sin once and for all had to be the blood of man.

Redemption was coming through God's Son, Jesus. He had planned it out perfectly and told all His prophets that a Savior was on the way. Every detail spoken through the mouthpieces of God prepared the way for those who listened. No information was held back regarding the Savior that was coming to redeem all the sins of the world. A loving father looked down at a broken world and decided that He was willing to become the sacrifice Himself for eternity. Elohim sent the Word to become flesh to pay the price for our disobedience.

Now that sin has been washed away by the blood of Lamb, does that mean that sin has been eradicated? No, sin still lives in the hearts and minds of men and women because we still live in this fallen world. Jesus made a way that cut through the laws and granted us full access to the Father. We still have a part to play, because forgiveness comes with repentance, which is sometimes our biggest obstacle.

Why is forgiveness so hard? Elton John sings about it in his song, "Sorry Seems to Be the Hardest Word." Like Elton John, Jesus wants to know what He has to do to make us love Him. The lyrics have new meaning when you hear them sung by Jesus. Imagine him singing to your heart that all will be forgiven. This beautiful visual packs a powerful punch. We don't like to see our flaws and think we can hide them from others. Asking for forgiveness from God and others means acknowledging those shortcomings. But pride refuses to submit and humble itself. We have been taught by fast-food chains and other worldly influences that we must have it our way. The Bible tells us the opposite and gives us the truth about the dangers of pride. Proverbs warns us, "Your boast becomes a prophecy of a future failure. The higher you lift yourself up in pride, the harder you'll fall in disgrace" (Proverbs 16:18). Feeding your ego will lead to the greatest fall.

Since the beginning, pride has played a huge part in falling away from God. Even before man was created, the angelic beings that surrounded the throne room all had free will to worship and serve Him. I love it that God doesn't demand us to do anything we don't want to do. Lucifer, the most beautiful of the angels, who was created to worship Elohim and was the orchestrator of all the sounds in heaven, fell because he wanted to be God.

Lucifer secretly desired the adoration that belonged to God, so a plan was set in motion, all because of jealousy. Pride had been given a seed. The definition of the word *pride*, according to *Merriam-Webster's Dictionary*, is "pleasure that comes from some relationship, association, achievement, or possession that is seen as a source of honor, respect, etc."[2] God revealed an acronym for pride:

Personal

Recognition

Invites

Doing

Evil.

When I saw that, it made sense that a lot of sin is rooted in pride.

Jesus came to earth to serve both God and man. He came without any reputation, according to the apostle Paul. "He existed in the form of God, yet he gave no thought to seizing equality with God as his supreme prize. Instead he emptied himself of his outward glory by reducing himself to the form of a lowly servant. He became human!" (Philippians 2:6–7). I love it when the Holy Spirit reveals a deeper understanding of the Word. Because Jesus did not have a reputation, He had nothing in Him to recognize. Jesus came to reveal the Father, and the Holy Spirit came to reveal the Son. No self-promotion, no jealousy, and no pride.

Many great leaders have lost their positions, and some, their lives, because they became more concerned about self than others. Jesus knew this weakness in man, so He chose to be selfless and show us the example of what true kingdom looks like. He came to teach us about honor, obedience, humility, and forgiveness; He came as the key to eternal life, opening a door of forgiveness for man, all through repentance.

Jesus was teaching in the synagogue when a woman was caught in adultery and thrown down before Him. (See John 8.) The Pharisees set this up to see if He would go against the law of Moses in Leviticus 20:10. Jesus says, "So when they continued asking Him, He raised Himself up and said to them, 'He who is without sin among you, let him throw a stone at her first'" (John 8:7 NKJV). We all carry some sin in us, and Jesus knew that when He spoke to the crowd that wanted to stone this woman. According to the law, both participants were supposed to be stoned, but they only brought out the woman.

The accuser of the brethren, the devil, keeps us in shame, guilt, and condemnation. The Pharisees wanted blood, and they wanted Jesus to be a part of it. Everyone was anxious to stone this woman, thinking they were fulfilling the law of God. They were all pointing out her sin, never realizing they had four fingers pointing back at their own sin. Jesus said He didn't come to change the law but to fulfill it. When Jesus called them out to confront their own sin, they had to drop their stones of judgment. "When Jesus had raised Himself up and saw no one but the woman, He said to her, 'Woman, where are those accusers of yours? Has no one condemned you?' She said, 'No one, Lord.' And Jesus said to her, 'Neither do I condemn you; go and sin no more'" (John 8:10–11 NKJV). The punishment of sin is death, and the enemy knows it. Jesus came to change it all by the blood. His blood blots out any and all sin as we come to Him freely in repentance. Every sin we confess to Jesus gives us the ability to choose to do it right the next time.

When children are playing a game and they are not quite prepared, they shout, "Do over!" If the odds are against them in an unfair situation, you will hear, "Do over," meaning, "I want a second chance to get this right, to be able to have another opportunity or a fair chance to succeed." Jesus is our "do over" every time we come to Him. He gives us both freedom and the ability to now have victory over our circumstances.

There is so much power in both repentance and forgiveness. The church has taught us well how we can go to Jesus and be made clean. The gospel songs of old speak of the power in the blood of Jesus that makes us white as snow. Jesus taught the disciples the principle of forgiveness through the parables of the prodigal son in Luke 15:11–32 and the unforgiving servant in Matthew 18:21–35.

Each of these parables gives a greater insight into how God looks at forgiveness. The prodigal son highlights the desire of a Father to redeem a broken relationship and a son who realizes that he can be forgiven for poor choices. Looking at this story, we can see our heavenly Father waiting with bated breath as His children are turning back to Him. The Father both accepts them and comes running to restore their relationship, authority, and inheritance.

In the story of the unforgiving servant, the king forgave any and all debt of the servant, only to find out that the servant would not forgive another. When the king found out, he locked up the servant and punished him for what he had done. God sent Jesus to forgive any and all sin that we committed, and in exchange, we are to do the same. Jesus said it very plainly: "And when you pray, make sure you forgive the faults of others so that your Father in heaven will also forgive you. But if you withhold forgiveness from others, your Father withholds forgiveness from you." (Matthew 6:14–15). As the saying goes, "Unforgiveness is like drinking poison yourself and waiting for the other person to die."[3] The enemy wants us to stay in unforgiveness and never repent because he then loses his grip on us.

We can't hide anything from God because He is all knowing. Three attributes of God are that He knows everything (omniscient), is everywhere at all times (omnipresent), and is all powerful (omnipotent), so why do we try to hide when we mess up?

God gives us a chance to change our minds before we take that left turn that leads us into sin. In Genesis 4, God has a heart-to-heart talk with Cain, one of the sons of Adam and Eve. Cain was a tiller of the ground, and their other son Abel was a keeper of sheep. They each brought offerings to God, but the Lord only respected Abel's offering. Cain was more concerned about the Lord recognizing his offering than about bringing what was required. "So the Lord said to Cain, 'Why are you angry? And why has your countenance fallen? If you do well, will you not be accepted? And if you do not do well, sin lies at the door. And its desire is for you, but you should rule over it'" (Genesis 4:6–7 NKJV). God knew that Cain was prideful and jealous and what he was planning in his heart and gave him a chance to change his mind. Cain still had an opportunity to repent from the wicked schemes of the evil he had prepared for his brother Abel.

Unfortunately, he had hardened his heart against his brother, and jealousy consumed him. Cain acted on the thoughts and then made them a reality. Cain's offering might not have been accepted because the ground he tilled was cursed. The only offering acceptable was a sheep, which foreshadows Jesus, the Lamb of God, who takes away the sin of the world. Cain was giving a defiled offering, and in his jealous rage, he took Abel out to the field and made him the blood sacrifice.

Cain operated in pride; his ego got the best of him. We can be as stubborn as Cain and refuse to acknowledge the right thing to do. In those pride-fueled moments, we miss the mark to become acceptable in the Lord's eyes. We give the enemy a place and space in our hearts when we refuse to repent or forgive. Just like Cain, the enemy begins knocking, hoping to unlock the evil that looms outside the door of sin. If we can't forgive others, then we are not forgiven, leaving us trapped in unrighteousness.

Many times, I have put up walls of unforgiveness due to the hurts or wounds left by others. As a child, I was once upset with a friend and told her that our friendship was over. I walked away but found my heart softened as the emotions slowly dissipated. We ran back to each other, saying sorry. That is the beauty of being a child: Anger is short-lived, and forgiveness comes easy. As we grow older, the offenses and hurts of the world leave a bigger sting, and the recovery often takes longer.

Many disappointments, wounds, trauma, abuse, rejections, and hurts held me captive. I accepted mistreatment from others, believing that I deserved it. As I let go of bad relationships and abuse, I never truly forgave anyone in my heart. Back when Facebook was the hottest social media platform, we wanted to be friends with everyone. We shared our stories and pictures, wanting to be seen and accepted. Slowly, new people showed up in our feeds as we began reconnecting with those from our past. Some of those faces inspired happy memories, and other names brought up unresolved fear as soon as we saw them.

I was often bullied in grammar and middle school by boys who thought I wasn't pretty enough or girls who thought I wasn't cool enough. We don't truly comprehend the damage we can do to others with our words and actions. Back then, I tried to stay under the radar as much as possible. In addition, a teacher bullied and ridiculed me, which didn't help matters; in fact, it made it acceptable for my peers to belittle me. The once outgoing little girl was slowly crumbling and forming the shell for a scared and introverted child to hide. No longer did I want to talk and share my stories; instead, I kept my humorous thoughts to myself. I had a few friends who I was comfortable with outside of school, but in school, my walls came back up.

It took me all of high school to shake off some of those traumas. As an adult, I finally learned that children can sometimes be mean. I was scrolling through Facebook when a name crossed my feed. Fear immediately surfaced. I quickly scrolled past the post, hoping none of my posts or comments were public. No way was I going to be bullied or ridiculed on Facebook. I drew a line in the proverbial sand and decided I would just not comment on anyone's post that they might know. The best solution was to stay hidden and unnoticed.

I had been in prayer with the Father and reading about forgiveness earlier that day. I asked Him how to know if I still had unforgiveness. The Father replied, "If you have any type of emotion connected to those memories, there is still unforgiveness." I went on with my day, but God was up to something. Later, I took a break from my daily chores and got on Facebook. As I was scrolling, I got a notification of a friend request from that person who triggered such angst. My heart felt as if it would beat out of my chest as the painful childhood memories flooded back. I sat there in disbelief as I stared at the name before me.

That familiar voice then said, "Well? Do you forgive them? Can you forgive them for the things they did as a child? Can you forgive them for not understanding how much that hurt you?" My racing mind whirled with every excuse not to forgive them for the pain, humiliation, suffering, trauma, and all the other hurts. I looked at the friend request as if it were waiting for a response, almost testing my Christianity. I closed my eyes, took a deep breath, and pushed accept. The tears began to fall as I released this person from any judgment I had held against them.

In that same moment, people's faces popped into my head as the Lord said, "Do you forgive them?" I didn't think of people on my own, but God was revealing the place in my heart where I had held them prisoner. The faces of those who caused me pain quickly disappeared with the words "I forgive them." Granting forgiveness brought another face and then another of the boys who teased me, the girls who bullied me, and the fair-weather friends who kicked me to the curb when I did not agree with them. The Holy Spirit was bringing me through this revolving door of memories as we shut each open door once and for all.

When this process ended, I sat there numb for a moment as the tears streamed down my face. And then it all lifted. It was all gone, including the fear that gripped me. No longer was I the victim; I was now free, and so were all those I held in captivity in my heart. The judgment was no longer mine but was now the Lord's. I had released my hand and put it in his hand. I didn't see everyone, because some hurts are not as simple to forgive; some take more time because they are deeper wounds.

We often blame the enemy for everything that goes wrong in life. Sometimes, we blame God for unanswered prayers or for events that seem out of our control. Through the entire thread of Scriptures, we see a common theme: God is good. His goodness and mercy are everlasting, and on that, we can depend. By turning to the Bible in times of trouble, we speak those Scriptures out loud that remind us of how truly good God is. They also remind us that God restores everything "To console those who mourn in Zion, to give them beauty for ashes, the oil of joy for mourning, the garment of praise for the spirit of heaviness; that they may be called trees of righteousness, the planting of the Lord, that He may be glorified" (Isaiah 61:3 NKJV). God has a way of making everything right.

Earlier, I mentioned that my mother was burned in a house fire and shared how God walked me through the entire ordeal. He held my hand and guided me every step of the way. But I didn't share why I fought so hard for my mom. She loved me and my siblings as much as she could. My grandfather was born in the United States and moved to Poland as a young man. My mother was then born and raised in Poland, went through World War II, and came to America when she was fourteen. She lived a very hard life and didn't have the nurturing that she should have had as a child. Her father and all the male members of her family were taken to a concentration camp during the Nazi invasion. Her mother's grandmothers raised her as my mom's mother tried to earn money to support the family. Like so many individuals, my mother suffered from abandonment, rejection, trauma, and father and mother wounds.

The expression "hurt people hurt people" is so true. If you have been so deeply wounded, it's hard not to affect others with your actions. It's like trying to hug a porcupine without getting poked. My mother loved and nurtured us to the degree she was loved and nurtured. Her father and her uncles were eventually released from the concentration camp once the war was over. The end of the war opened a door for him and his family to leave Poland, return to the US, and start a new life.

My mom was the last member of her family that came over by boat. She was enrolled in elementary school although she was a teenager and stayed in school just long enough to learn English. She met my dad at a local drugstore, drinking a soda while reading an *Archie* comic book. They married quickly before he was deployed by the Navy. A year later, my brother Rik entered the world, and eleven years later, I was born on his birthday. My sister, Tina, arrived three years after me, and finally my youngest brother, David, completed our family three years later. My family was filled with dysfunction and lots of anger. My siblings and I sort of raised ourselves because my mom would check out and leave us emotionally and physically. The lack of security of a mom who was there for me left a big hole in my heart.

I was always looking for a mother to fill that place, only to be disappointed with the mothering figures who came in and out of my life. But when I met my future husband, I hit the jackpot. My future mother-in-law was everything I ever wanted in a mom. She was active in her community, had a ton of friends, was very respected by all who knew her, dressed to the nines, and had impeccable taste. Yep, she was the perfect version of the mother I had envisioned since my youth, and she would become a real mom to me through marriage. Even before my wedding day, my future mom and I did all kinds of things together: shopped, attended a taping of *Live! With Regis and Kathie Lee* (her favorite program at the time), went to concerts and musicals, talked for hours, and more.

Because of the time we spent together, she was quickly becoming my best friend. She taught me how to entertain and cook and become the mom I had always wanted to be but never knew how. We had the greatest relationship, and I loved her because she filled that hole perfectly.

That same year when my mother was burned in the house fire, my father-in-law was in the same hospital, suffering with congestive heart failure. The day my mother was airlifted to the hospital, my mother-in-law was coming to visit her husband. I was a wreck as I sat in the lobby, trying to be strong for my family and trying to imagine what my life would look like without my mother in it. I was trying to hold it together, but it was becoming increasingly difficult. Due to the seriousness of her burn injuries, the doctor told me it would be touch-and-go for the next few days.

Sorrow and fear were bubbling up, and I needed the arms of mother to wrap around me and tell me it would all be okay. Right then, my in-law's car pulled around the front of the hospital to park. I could finally get the comfort I so desperately needed. As my mother-in-law approached the glass doors, my heart quickened. The tears welled up in my eyes as I rushed over to her. My words broken, I began to embrace her. I barely choked out, "M-o-m," when something shifted. Instead of pulling me in, she grabbed my hand and held me at a distance.

She looked at me strangely as she asked what happened. My mind reeled. She didn't know! I told her my mom was in a house fire with burns over 50 percent of her body. My mother-in-law asked, "And what else?"

I said that my mom had suffered third- and fourth-degree burns and they had to airlift her to the hospital. Again, she asked, "Is there anything else?"

I continued to tell her that my mom was put into a medically induced coma, her lungs were severely burned, and we were not sure if she would make it. My mother-in-law looked me in the eyes, shook my hand, and said, "Okay, okay then," still keeping me at a distance. She released my hand as the familiar coldness of rejection reached out to clutch my heart. I thought that she was the one, the mom who would love me and be there for me. I swallowed back the tears and shook off the disappointment of yet another woman who had decided I was not worthy of love. The comfort I so desperately now needed would have to wait until I could lie in my bed, wrapped in a blanket that would have to substitute for a person.

I took her upstairs to see my mom in the ICU burn unit. I was quiet as we walked through the doors into her room. The nurse was adjusting her medicine and explaining what procedures had already been done. I asked him if he thought she would be okay. He smiled. "Let's just take it one day at a time."

We left the ICU and went to see my father-in-law. We carried on a light conversation, but I still couldn't process what had happened. My visit with my father-in-law was short as I needed to find my dad and meet my siblings who were traveling to New Jersey. I walked to the elevator, completely numb. I was losing my birth mother, and my mother-in-law would no longer fill that void. The old wounds from all the mother figures in my life who had decided I was not good enough to call "daughter" erupted. I couldn't figure out what I had done wrong. Why was she now so cold toward me? Maybe I scared her, and she thought that her husband had taken a turn for the worse. Perhaps I was too emotional, and she didn't know how to handle it.

No matter the reason, I had believed a lie that she truly loved me like a daughter. I was on a rollercoaster of emotions with all the triggers of past hurts. My mother-in-law had no idea how badly she had hurt me, but the damage was done. And so was I. I began to erect walls in my heart that day, and I secretly said goodbye to any chance of ever having a true healthy mother-and-daughter relationship. The brokenness, dismissal, and rejection were simply too much for me to handle, and so I shut down that part of my heart for good.

With that revelation, I began praying and begging the Lord to heal my mom. Even with all the drama, she loved me. In the moments she was present, she cared and showed me affection. I needed my mom and her hugs. I didn't want to lose her and was not willing to let her go without a fight. Something rose up inside me, and a warrior emerged. The devil tried to take my mom, but now he would have to go through me to get to her. I would pray the hardest and longest prayers to fix this. A new love for her rose within me.

As I previously shared, my mother was, in fact, healed and released from the hospital. I got my mom back, but I struggled with my relationship with my mother-in-law from that day on. Only a few weeks later, my father-in-law would graduate to heaven, and my mother-in-law would lose her very best friend. As the years passed, we were cordial with each other, but the close friendship we had was now distant. The hurt I carried had turned me cold, and the judgment of everything she did was getting easier as my heart became more hardened toward her.

It would take a move of God to repair the rips and tears of my heart due to rejection, and that was exactly what He intended to do. As some folks say, He is Jehovah Sneaky, and I certainly encountered Him in that way.

My kids were involved in Pop Warner football and cheer that fall. My daughter was in a cheerleading competition, and it was a very big deal to go and cheer her on. I was doing the dishes when a small voice told me to invite my mother-in-law to the competition that was taking place in a few weeks. My response was, "Sure I will, Lord." I thought that she would decline the invitation, because it would mean spending the night at our house.

I casually mentioned it to my husband, and he thought it was a great idea. He called his mom, and much to my surprise, she was excited to come and stay with us. Ugh, Jehovah Sneaky was definitely up to something, but what it was, I had no idea.

The day arrived for her visit. Once again, we had a superficial conversation as I prepared our dinner. We chatted about what she was doing, and then we began talking about God. (Jehovah Sneaky was on the move.) I shared some new Bible stories and encouragement from our pastor. The conversation turned to the sermons by Pastor Joel Osteen; apparently, she was tuning in to watch him on Sunday mornings. At the time, I, too, was listening to Joel and was so excited to discuss some of the stories he had shared. We had a lovely dinner and continued to talk until bedtime. We turned in early, because we needed to be up super early for the Saturday morning competition.

The next morning, we hurried out the door so that we could be on time for check-in. My daughter was taken to her squad as we found seats to watch the competition. This was her first real competition, so the emotions were running high as the girls performed their routine. The squad did such a great job and moved on to the next level, scheduled for later in the season. We were all exhausted from the early wake up and the excitement of the event.

I would have preferred to go out to breakfast, but instead, we decided to go home. I stopped by the grocery store, grumbling and complaining that I now had to make breakfast for everyone. Once home, I quickly whipped up a meal, cleaned up, and went to my bedroom for a break. I called my friend and asked her to please call me back and invite me over as I just could not take it. I was angry that I had to cook, entertain, clean, or be engaging. A few minutes later, the phone rang with my friend's invitation, and I was released from the prison. I couldn't wait to dump all my frustrations on my friend and reveal how I really felt about my mother-in-law. We chatted all night, and I complained about everything until it was time to leave.

The next morning, I woke up as the Lord said, "Go get your mother-in-law coffee at Dunkin."

I flippantly responded, "No, I'm not going to get her coffee. Instead, I will make it." I knew she preferred Dunkin and it was a treat for her, but I only wanted to get through this day as quickly as I could. I went to the kitchen to make coffee, but the coffee filter was nowhere to be found. I needed coffee, stat.

My mother-in-law came in as I was still searching. She said, "Hey, why don't you run over to Dunkin for some coffee and donuts? My treat." Ugh, Jehovah Sneaky strikes again!

I came back with the hot coffee and donuts for the kids. It was Sunday, so we watched Joel Osteen before getting ready for the football game. The charismatic preacher with the huge smile shared stories and Scriptures. We both perked up. I started to share some of the messages from other preachers when she decided it was time to get ready for the game. The kids were heading to the kitchen as Grandma was passing out the donuts and pouring OJ. I sat back and took a sip of coffee when the Lord said, "Lisa, go and apologize to your mother-in-law."

A jolt shot through me at the injustice of this request. "What! Are you kidding me? Do you not see what she has done to me?" I heard nothing back, and so I thought, *Good, I must have pleaded my case, so now God must agree with me.*

My mother-in-law walked past me on her way to get dressed. The kids were now finishing up their donuts and getting ready for the game as well. Once again, the Lord spoke. "Lisa, go and apologize to your mother-in-law."

Now I was angry. "No way. She is the one who should be apologizing to me for how she hurt me. She rejected me, remember? I'm the one hurting, not her. She has not been nice to me." I figured that should silence any more suggestions from God.

Nope. For the third time, the Lord said, "Lisa, go and apologize to your mother-in-law." I knew at that point, He wouldn't let this go. I decided not to argue but to try to figure out a way to get this over and done with. I thought she was styling her hair in the bathroom. The door was ajar, and so I peeked in, but she was not there.

Well, she isn't here, so I did what you wanted. My job is done, right? I began to brush my teeth when I had a vision of talking to my mother-in-law. I began crying as she opened her arms, grabbed me, and held me. Then the vision ended. I shook my head. That thought couldn't be from God, because she didn't hug or comfort anyone. I was about to leave the bathroom when I noticed her sweater.

I picked up the sweater and went to her bedroom. I knocked on the door and asked to come in. After she agreed, I closed the door behind me to signal to the kids that they should not bother us. I handed her the sweater and asked if I could talk to her. She nodded. "What do you want to talk about?"

I swallowed and looked at her. "Mom, I want to apologize for how I have been treating you."

She responded, "I don't know what you are talking about."

I thought, *Oh Lord, she is not going to make this easy, is she?* I said, "Well, I have not been very kind to you lately, and I feel like we are not as close as we used to be."

She said, "Well, I have not gone anywhere or done anything to make that happen." This time, this superficial apology was turning into the real deal. From my heart, I began to share the sadness of our broken relationship and how I no longer wanted that. I wanted to go back to the way we once were. Then I began to cry.

I'm not exactly sure how it happened, but through the tears and sobbing of how I wanted to fix our relationship, two arms began pulling me in. Her perfume wafted around me as she told me it would be okay. I hugged her back, and we agreed the feud was over. I gave her a kiss on her check, and she smiled back as she told me to get ready. We had the best day, cheering on the kids as they cheered and played football. We ate a quick lunch before my mother-in-law headed back home. Saying goodbye was different this time as real love flowed as we hugged.

The next day, my friend called, asking how the rest of the weekend went. I told her some of the stories that normally would have brought up anger and resentment, but they didn't. In fact, those negative feelings were now gone. All of them just seemed to vanish as if I couldn't remember how to be angry at my mother-in-law anymore. It was a weird feeling as freedom was again finding a place in my heart. I asked the Lord what had happened. He told me that I asked for forgiveness, and it was granted. I also forgave my mother-in-law, so now, nothing was holding me hostage to anger. I told Him, "You set me up, didn't you?"

The Lord then explained why He did what He did. "Lisa, you were ready to let go of the anger. It wasn't that your mother-in-law didn't love you. She didn't reject you. It was because of me. I had her reject you so that you would pray for your mother. You needed to fight for your mother's life, and if you had the support of your mother-in-law, you would have let your mom go." I sat there shaking my head as the Lord spoke. "Lisa, that hug that she denied you so many years ago was given to you yesterday. That's why you needed to ask for forgiveness, because you really needed that hug!"

FORGIVENESS AND REPENTING:

Heavenly Father, I humbly come before you, asking you to forgive me for anything I may have done or said that did not bring glory to you. Father, forgive me for my disobedience or for choosing my way instead of your way. Lord, I ask you to cleanse me with the blood of your Son, Jesus Christ, and wash me clean. I repent for my earthly ways, and I choose to walk in your heavenly ways. Holy Spirit, I ask you to make me quick to repent, quick to forgive. I ask you to protect and guard my heart so it doesn't become hardened. Thank you, Lord, that you forgive me. Help me forgive others the way that you have forgiven me. Help me not to judge, mock, or cause anyone to stumble. Keep my heart and motives pure. Holy Spirit, I ask you to reveal any wrong in my heart or actions. I ask you now to reveal anyone that I have not forgiven. I release to you anyone and everyone who I have held in judgment. I thank you, Jesus, that because of you, I have been forgiven. I ask you to help me forgive myself, and I forgive myself for any and all mistakes that I have made. I thank you, Jesus, for your blood that has washed me clean. I thank you for the healing of my soul and the restoration of my heart. I give you all glory and honor, in Jesus's name. Amen.

CHAPTER 11

Authority, Agreement, and Declarations

Now you understand that I have imparted to you my authority to trample over his kingdom. You will trample upon every demon before you and overcome every power Satan possesses. Absolutely nothing will harm you as you walk in this authority.

~ Luke 10:19

In the beginning, God created man and woman to rule over the earth, the fish of the sea, the birds of the air, and every living creature, according to Genesis 1:26. Man was given the authority of dominion by the Creator of the heavens, and we were created to have sovereignty over the earth. As soon as God gave man this authority, the devil came in to steal it. The devil or satan wanted to be the ruler of this world, so he devised a plan that would allow him access to man. The fall of man gave the devil dominion over this world.

In the wilderness, Jesus was tempted for forty days by the devil and was offered everything that the devil had the authority to give.

The devil lifted Jesus high into the sky, and in a flash showed him all the kingdoms and regions of the world. The devil then said to Jesus, "All of this, with all its power, authority, and splendor, is mine to give to whomever I wish. Just do one thing, and you will have it all. Simply bow down to worship me, and it will be yours! You will possess everything!" (Luke 4:5–7)

The enemy could not give away anything that he didn't have the right to offer. God knew that he had to give back to man what had been taken, but this had to be a legal transaction. If an open door of sin gave the devil access, then the removal of sin would close that door once and for all. Jesus says, "From this moment on, everything in this world is about to change, for the ruler of this dark world will be overthrown" (John 12:31). God's redemption plan was now set into action to bring back the original design of man to rule and reign over this world. With His blood, Jesus bought back everything that was stolen and gave it back to us.

Then Jesus came close to them and said, "All authority of the universe has been given to me. Now wherever you go, make disciples of all nations, baptizing them in the name of the Father, the Son, and the Holy Spirit. And teach them to faithfully follow all that I have commanded you. And never forget that I am with you every day, even to the completion of this age." (Matthew 28:18–20)

The authority is ours and has been purchased for us at a great cost. Many believers in Jesus still have not comprehended the magnitude of power we have as sons and daughters of God, in covenant with Him. The twelve disciples were sent out to preach the gospel, but before they left, Jesus commissioned them. "Then He called His twelve disciples together and gave them power and authority over all demons, and to cure diseases" (Luke 9:1 NKJV). When they returned, they marveled that demons had to obey them.

Some movies about exorcisms make it seem as if the devil is stronger than God. The power the demons had over the person makes it seem as if the priests didn't have the authority or the strength to tell them to leave. These movies make it look as if the devil is winning until the very end. Hollywood has glamorized the devil and his power. No wonder Christians are afraid of him or, worse, don't believe he actually exists. If they only knew that they carried Jesus inside them.

My friend Tyler Johnson was preaching at a small church in Pennsylvania, so I invited my friend to go with me. As we walked in, much to our surprise, the worship was videos of popular Christian worship songs. We found a place to sit and began to worship. I started to have a vision of all of us dancing in the water. The strong presence of God was released as all His children were gathered, praising His name. The music changed, and so did my vision.

I was now dancing with Jesus in this ballroom, wearing a beautiful white dress and waltzing around the room. Jesus began to spin me, and we both were laughing when demons suddenly approached the dance floor. I hid behind Jesus as He turned to face them. He put both of His hands on His hips and squared His shoulders just like Superman does. The demons quickly fled, and we began dancing again. As the music swayed, a sash, like you see in a beauty pageant, descended from heaven. The beautiful red sash fell on me and draped over my shoulder and hung around my waist. There was no writing on it, but the color contrasted with my white dress. A gold-and-diamond crown appeared on my head as we continued dancing.

I felt like a princess dancing with my King Jesus. We were moving as one as the music played. Once again, those pesky demons returned to interrupt our dance. This time, Jesus didn't confront those demons. I did. Following my teacher, I turned and looked at those demons with both hands on my hips and posing with the same stance as Jesus had done. The demons fled, just like they did earlier. Angels came over to us and bowed before me. Frantically, I said, "No, no, no! Do not bow to me!"

Jesus chuckled. "Lisa, they are not bowing to you but to the sash, which is made of my blood. They are bowing to the blood. You are wearing my banner." With that, the vision ended.

I sat in silence as I tried to process at what I had witnessed. The Lord then whispered, "Yahweh-Nissi, the Lord is our banner." God revealed this name to Moses as he was fighting the Amalekites. As long as Moses had his staff held up, the Israelites would win, but as he dropped his staff, they would begin losing. So his brother Aaron and Hur, a member of the tribe of Judah, held up the hands of Moses to bring the victory to the Israelites. (See Exodus 17.)

After the battle, God instructed Moses to write it all down, and then he built an altar named Jehovah-Nissi, the Lord is our banner. Just like Moses had the staff of God, I now had a banner draped over me in the spirit, reminding me that the battle is the Lord's. Jesus came to show us the true power and authority we have in Him and His blood. At the name of Jesus, every knee shall bow and every tongue will proclaim that He is Lord of all. (See Philippians 2:10–11.) When Jesus went to the cross, He gave us each a blood-soaked banner to wear in the spirit, letting the enemy know his time is done.

As a new believer, I was petrified of the devil, and thoughts of demons were too terrifying to imagine. The Holy Spirit began to show me the truth of deliverance as another way of healing and facing my fear. The first time I ever confronted a demon was while ministering at a women's retreat for a Spanish ministry. I had an interpreter by my side. When it was time for prayer, the ladies were told to line up. I began to pray over each one, and the minute my hands came down, the women would begin crying. Thirty women were all waiting for prayer, and soon as I touched them, the tears would start.

After I prayed for about ten women, the heat began to intensify, especially on my arms. I felt as if a piece of wood were placed across my shoulders as I approached this young lady. My hands raised above her head and slowly started to lower over her shoulders. As soon as I touched her, she shrieked loudly and fell to the floor. Her hands began to twist as if she were having a seizure. Her eyes rolled up in her head, and her tongue became pointy like a lizard's. She started to slither on the ground like a snake. I took a quick step back as I was unprepared, but my friend who came with me ran to her. My friend began shouting the name of Jesus, and the girl turned, cursed at my friend, and continued slithering. Now I got mad because you don't talk to my friends like that, and we commanded that thing to leave. The woman came back to herself, and I continued ministering to the rest of the women.

The pastors never came over to assist me nor did they seem shocked by the demonic manifestation. The next day, I shared my experience with my spiritual father, and he simply said, "Welcome to ministry!"

My first few encounters with demons were filled with fear and trepidation. I have since learned a lot more about authority and how we actually have great jurisdiction over the powers of darkness. After many interviews with various guests on *Touched by Prayer*, I learned how to use my authority over the demonic. These mighty men and women of God understood their truth and identity as children of God. Through their testimonies and teachings, I began to understand that we have been allowing the enemy to rule over us instead of us ruling over them.

I was invited back to another women's conference at the same Spanish church. This time, I was prepared as I began to preach and teach about forgiveness. The ladies came up for prayer, and I was not giving any demon the opportunity to show themselves. I began to pray over a woman, and the interpreter was sharing what the

Holy Spirit was revealing to me. I told her it was time to let go of unforgiveness toward her husband, but she was not receiving it at all. As soon as I started to tell her to forgive, the woman began heaving as if she were about to throw up.

The leadership team recognized that this was a deliverance and ran over with a bag for the woman to throw up in. Right then, a holy anger rose within me. I spoke to that spirit that wanted to humiliate her and shouted, *"You will not speak, act, or manifest in my presence!"* I pointed at the bag and said, "Get that bag away!" Immediately, she turned around. This deliverance would be vomit-free.

I went back to ministering to the woman who didn't speak much English and told the interpreter that she needed to forgive her husband. As the interpreter translated, she again began to manifest, dry heaving. The woman with the plastic bag again came running. I spoke to the spirit yet again and commanded it not to speak, act, or manifest. I then turned to the woman with the bag, pointing that she should take it away.

This happened one more time until I finally told the interpreter that until the woman forgave her husband, this spirit would not let her go. The woman was now in tears, and I gently said, "You need to forgive to be free."

She screamed as she slowly fell to her knees. I followed her down to the ground when she said, "Perdonar," which means *forgive* in Spanish. As soon as she did, the spirit began to manifest and just like before, it had to obey my commands. The defeated spirit spit on the floor. The team rushed over to wipe it up. I could now cast it out because it lost its legal right to stay in the woman. I pulled up the once tormented woman. She smiled, her face glowing in her newfound freedom. She hugged and thanked me.

I told her, "Don't thank me. Thank Jesus." She nodded and looked up to heaven, kissing the air as if blowing a kiss to the King of Kings.

Some demons are hard of hearing, so you might need to raise your voice. We use this same tone when sternly reprimanding a pet or child, a different tone that is reserved when you are stepping into an authoritative role. In healing as well as deliverance, the understanding of who and whose you are makes the difference. Jesus tells the disciples, "Listen to the truth I speak to you: Whoever says to this mountain with great faith and does not doubt, 'Mountain, be lifted up and thrown into the midst of the sea,' and believes that what he says will happen, it will be done" (Mark 11:23). So many believe the lie that our words don't matter, but Jesus says what we say with our mouths and with great faith will be accomplished. The enemy does not want you to understand how very mighty you are as a believer in Jesus. We carry His authority. In addition, through the covenant, we can declare what will be established.

We need to be careful what we say because of the power we hold in our tongue and in our words. "Death and life are in the power of the tongue, and those who love it will eat its fruit" (Proverbs 18:21 NKJV). When the Lord began talking to me about declaring and establishing His desires, He was serious. He showed me that before anything was established, He used man to speak it out. God used the prophet Elijah to decree things to people, including the woman from Zarephath.

And Elijah said to her, "Do not fear; go and do as you have said, but make me a small cake from it first, and bring it to me; and afterward make some for yourself and your son. For thus says the Lord God of Israel: 'The bin of flour shall not be used up, nor shall the jar of oil run dry, until the day the Lord sends rain on the earth.'" So she went away and did according to the word of Elijah; and she and he and her household ate for many days. The bin of flour was not used up, nor did the jar of oil run dry, according to the word of the Lord which He spoke by Elijah. (1 Kings 17:13–16 NKJV)

It had to be spoken before it could be established.

I have prophesied different events, not realizing that what I was saying was making a way in the spirit. For example, I went to visit my friend Tatyana at her new gym. She had only moved a week or so earlier. It was her first gym and was specifically for personal training. She only had enough room for one or two people. She was so excited to be branching out into her own business after working for another gym. Tatyana came to America from Uzbekistan, looking to live the American dream. I met Taty at church one day. God told me to go and pray over her. I didn't know much about her except she loved Jesus. You could see it all over her as she served as an usher.

I walked into her gym, looked at her with a big smile, and told her, "Don't put too much money into this place. God has a bigger place for you." Within six months, Tatyana moved into a bigger gym. She became my personal trainer and one of my best friends. We would pray together, and I would share my crazy God stories as I worked out. Her greatest prayer request was that her daughter would come to live with her.

We prayed for her to get her green card, which was the first step in getting Ravina to America. The day we prayed, I asked if her husband was trying to come too. (He had previously been deported back to Russia.) She said, "No, I don't think he can come, because he was deported."

I began crying as I told her that God would reunite the family, and both her husband and daughter would be coming. We hugged and cried as the word of Lord struck her heart with hope. Less than a year later, both her husband and daughter would arrive at JFK

Airport. God's word had been declared, and the moment it was spoken, it started to act.

Taty's faith had grown so much that she began to pray for everything. I was working out with her one morning when she began to complain about a mole that had appeared suddenly. She asked me if I would pray it away. We finished my workout and went back to her office. I put my hand on the mole, and she felt a burning heat. God was present, and He would not disappoint His daughter. In the same way Jesus spoke to the fig tree, I began declaring that mole was not allowed on Tatyana's face. "And seeing a fig tree by the road, He came to it and found nothing on it but leaves, and said to it, 'Let no fruit grow on you ever again.' Immediately the fig tree withered away" (Matthew 21:19 NKJV).

I told that mole to shrivel up and die in the name of Jesus. I pulled back my finger. The color of the mole was no longer a dark brown but a lighter skin tone. But some of the darker pigment was still there, and it looked like a weird face. I told Tatyana, "Your mole is giving me a stink eye." With that, we both burst out laughing as the joy of the Lord hit us. I prayed, "I cut off all blood to your root system, and you will drop off, leaving no scar."

Tatyana said, "Lisa, I feel something happening." We began thanking the Father for His goodness and Jesus for His stripes that heal us.

The next day, Taty told me that the mole was very dry. She touched it, and pieces of it came off. Seven days later (seven is the number for completion), that mole would not only fall completely off but not leave a scar. It was as if it were never there. She marveled at this, but I reminded her that we had declared that it would drop off her face. That is the power we have in our declarations and when we pray in agreement.

I often tell people, "Be careful who you pray with, because what you come into agreement with, you will see come to fruition." Jesus taught this principal to His disciples. "Again, I give you an eternal truth: If two of you agree to ask God for something in a symphony of prayer, my heavenly Father will do it for you" (Matthew 18:19).There is power in agreement.

The day after Thanksgiving 2020, I was drinking my coffee, scrolling through Facebook when a friend, Michelle, sent a message to our group. She lived in Texas, and we had met at a worship gathering in DC. This woman was a powerhouse prayer warrior. She was looking for someone who would pray with her for her friend's daughter. I wrote back, "I will pray with you." Immediately, my phone rang as she began to tell me that another person who was praying had lost the faith to continue. Kayman, the eighteen-year-old daughter of one of her best friends, had been in a car accident and suffered a traumatic brain injury. She had been in a coma for two weeks, and Michelle believed that God would heal her. I told her, "Okay, let's pray." As I wrote earlier, I have had some success praying for people in comas.

As soon as we started to pray, I heard in my spirit and told Michelle, "Well, it looks like we are going to heaven." My spirit engaged as we entered a beautiful garden in heaven. A young lady was walking with Jesus, His arm gently holding her close as they were having a serious discussion. I asked my friend if the girl had light-brown hair because I didn't know what she looked like and I wanted to be sure I was seeing correctly.

She replied, "No, she is a dark blonde, but do you see the black-and-white dog?" I told her to hold on, and I looked down. Sure enough, I saw the dog.

"Is the dog like a black-and-white cocker spaniel?"

She shouted, "Yes!"

As I focused on Kayman and Jesus, I didn't see their lips moving but could hear this heart-to-heart conversation. She was concerned about coming back to earth because she didn't think she would fully recover. She struggled with worry and trepidation, knowing that she had a choice to make. Jesus stopped walking with her and told her that she would both recover and that every milestone she made would bring other people to Him.

I shared what was revealed to me with Michelle, and we began to pray to break off fear and worry. The Holy Spirit revealed to me that Kayman was not on life support and that she had suffered no internal injuries. My friend got so excited as all I was sharing was true. The Holy Spirit downloaded more information, which was confirmed to be accurate. Just then, Liz, the mother of this girl, called Michelle, so she asked me if we could do a three-way phone call. Within seconds, Liz was on the phone.

Liz told us a member of the hospital staff had told her that they could do nothing more for her daughter. She now had to find a long-term facility to take her daughter who would remain in a coma. This person said the chances of her daughter waking up after this long seemed impossible, and if she did wake up, she would suffer long-term brain damage. In other words, the hospital believed she would never recover.

My friend asked me to share all that I had seen in heaven, and as I was sharing these details, I began to prophesy. I declared the destiny of Kayman and the plans that God had for her. The mother was in tears as I was sharing the same dreams that her daughter had spoken about to her. The mother shared how her daughter loved Jesus and people. I asked her if they had a black-and-white cocker spaniel.

She replied, "I'm not sure."

Confused, I asked, "You're not sure? Did you have a black-and-white dog that looks like a cocker spaniel?" Liz said that they had a black-and-white rescue puppy that her daughter loved, but it fallen into the pool and drowned. Kayman was heartbroken and kept a picture of the puppy in her bedroom.

Suddenly, I was brought back to heaven as Kayman hugged Jesus goodbye. I began shouting, "She is coming back! She is coming back today! She is hugging Jesus goodbye!" We all were in tears at this update from heaven, and we all began to pray. We declared that she would fully recover and walk out all the plans and purposes that God had for her. We believed this was a done deal. The prayers of a mother were powerful, and now three mommas were praying for a miracle. Our prayer was of remembrance of all the promises written in the Bible, the declaration of what we wanted established, the words of knowledge spoken that assured us God was in it, the faith that was rising inside us all, and unity as we interceded.

Before we hung up, I asked Liz to keep us updated. She agreed and thanked me for interceding for her baby girl. I told her, "Of course. We'll be in touch." I sat for a few minutes and thanked God for His goodness and faithfulness. I got up and began pulling out my Christmas decorations. I checked my phone throughout the day to see if I had any updates. But nothing.

By 2:30 p.m., I still hadn't heard anything from Michelle or Liz. I sat on the couch and began to pray to the Father in the spirit. Then I began crying. My heart was breaking for this mother as her daughter lay beside her. "If I was wrong, or if it was my imagination, you need to tell me. I will call them and tell them I got it wrong. I will tell them it was my imagination, but please don't let this mother have a false hope. Don't let her believe something that isn't true. I'm so sorry if I got it wrong, and I'm willing to make this right. Please, Papa, you need to let me know." Right then, I was taken back to heaven and to the garden. Jesus was smiling and walking with just the dog.

I began to praise God and knew that this would really happen. I texted the ladies. Okay, let's put a demand on this, and ask for a time. God, we ask that she wakes up by 3:33 pm. I hit the send button and added a heart sticker and got hearts back.

I prayed and looked at my phone. It was now 3:40 p.m., and still nothing. I continued praying and told God, "I picked 3:33 because it was a good number, Papa." I thought I got it wrong when, right around 4:33, I got the text from the mother and a video with her daughter responding to commands to squeeze her mother's hand. I began crying as I realized that they lived in Texas—where it was now exactly 3:33 p.m. Her daughter woke that day just as we declared. We had to contend for a few weeks as the hospital was not convinced that she was truly awake. Every negative report they spoke, we canceled and declared the opposite. She was eventually released and went home to be with her family.

I flew out to Texas four months later and met Kayman in person, the same girl I saw in heaven. I prayed over her and declared that all that Jesus promised her in heaven, she would see fulfilled here on earth. Liz, Michelle, and I all agreed, and so did Kayman.

As of the writing of this book in November 2022, Kayman is making progress every day. She's talking in complete sentences and can actually tell us a little about heaven.

Authority, Agreement, and Declarations:

Heavenly Father, I thank you that because of your Son, Jesus Christ, I have been given authority over demons, sickness, and all things here on earth. Lord, forgive me for thinking that the enemy has more authority than I do. Lord, I pick up my sword that says that I am ruling and reigning as a child of the most high God. I thank you, Lord, that you have given me authority and that where I walk, Jesus walks with me. I thank you that wherever two or more of us are in agreement, that you are there in our midst. I thank you that the agreements that we make here on earth are the agreements that you've already made in heaven. I thank you, Lord, that as we decree and declare, that it will be established. Help me be bold as I speak with authority and come into agreement with your plans and purposes. Let my words be a declaration of what you need established, and may everything be done for your glory and honor in Jesus's name. Amen.

CHAPTER 12

Love

Our love for others is our grateful response to the love God first demonstrated to us.

~ 1 John 4:19

The Beatles had it right when they sang "All You Need Is Love." We were created in the image of God. "So God created man in His own image; in the image of God He created him; male and female He created them" (Genesis 1:27 NKJV). But what is the image of God? According to 1 John 4:16, God is love, and God loved us so much, He sent His Son Jesus to give us everlasting life as written in John 3:16.

Throughout the Bible, we can see the love of our Creator in heaven who, time and time again, loves us in spite of what we do. From Genesis to Revelation, the Bible is the greatest love story ever told. The redeeming love written through the experiences of the fathers of the faith gives us a small understanding of what perfect love can do.

In the New Testament, we see a firsthand account of how love wrapped itself in flesh to put a very broken world back together. The Father, Son, and Holy Spirit were on a search-and-destroy mission. They came to search the hearts of men and women who yearned to return to the family. Jesus was sent to those who cried out to God to take them back, and the Holy Spirit came to give them assurance they were accepted. The strategies of the enemy were nothing but a distraction to keep man from understanding the great love that God offered us.

Conversations with diverse people have shown me that many have looked at God with a skewed perception of who He is. They see the Father as a mean and tyrannical God who demands obedience, or people will suffer the consequences. I have read the Scriptures and see a very loving and compassionate Father who is desperately trying to win back the affection of His children. If He is love, then how could He be anything other than that? Yet so many have been blinded by fear that they don't recognize His love.

The story of Abraham sacrificing his son Isaac is only one example people have used to prove that God is cruel. (See Genesis 22.) I, too, have misunderstood this story. But we must understand the nature and character of a loving Father. The Canaanites dwelled in the land where the Lord sent Abraham. The people who lived there worshipped the false gods of Baal and Molech. They offered their children as the highest praise of sacrifice to these false gods. This was how they acquired wealth and security and appeased their pagan gods. Abraham understood the demand those gods placed on their people. When the Lord asked Abraham to sacrifice His only son, he was familiar with the practice, so he accepted this request. However, consider these major differences.

First, God told Abraham that Isaac carried the seed of all the generations inside him. If he died, there would be no other descendants. Second was the faith that Abraham had in God because he knew this God to be faithful to His word. Abraham takes his son and tells his servants this: "Stay here with the donkey; the lad and I will go yonder and worship, and we will come back to you" (Genesis 22:5 NKJV). Abraham already knew that whatever happened on that mountain, God would not let his son die. He knew that this God had great power and would preserve his son to ensure his inheritance. Lastly, God gave Abraham a suitable sacrifice. "Then Abraham lifted his eyes and looked, and there behind him was a ram caught in a thicket by its horns. So Abraham went and took the ram, and offered it up for a burnt offering instead of his son" (Genesis 22:13 NKJV). Here, God revealed His name of Jehovah-Jireh, "the Lord will provide." "And Abraham called the name of the place, The-Lord-Will-Provide; as it is said to this day, In the Mount of the Lord it shall be provided'" (Genesis 22:14 NKJV). This is a foreshadow of Jesus the Lamb that was sent as the perfect sacrifice for all sin.

I always had an issue with this whole story because I didn't see God's love. How could a loving God ask for your child to be sacrificed just to prove you love Him? But the Father provided a sacrifice instead of demanding one, which proved He was different than those other gods. He was now known as the God of Abraham, Isaac, and Jacob, because He set Himself apart from the other gods. He was the God who would not demand a human sacrifice. He was the God that would bless man and would eventually provide the highest possible sacrifice, His own Son.

God is a giver and not a taker. He is self-sufficient; He needs nothing. In Him is completeness, so He can give freely to His children. God is just and righteous; He is fair and always does what is right. He is merciful and compassionate, and most of all, God is good. The goodness of God passed before Moses on Mt. Sinai. "Then He said, 'I will make all My goodness pass before you, and I will proclaim the name of the Lord before you. I will be gracious to whom I will be gracious, and I will have compassion on whom I will have compassion'" (Exodus 33:19 NKJV). The holiness of God was revealed to man once again as He passed before Moses. Moses only saw God's back, which changed his face, because seeing God face-to-face would have killed Moses. The love and friendship God had for Moses was so strong that He wanted to protect him, so the Lord hid him in a rock. The only way to keep Moses safe was to hide him inside Jesus, the Rock.

According to Paul, Jesus is the rock. "Moreover, brethren, I do not want you to be unaware that all our fathers were under the cloud, all passed through the sea, all were baptized into Moses in the cloud and in the sea, all ate the same spiritual food, and all drank the same spiritual drink. For they drank of that spiritual Rock that followed them, and that Rock was Christ" (1 Corinthians 10:1–4 NKJV). We are hidden in Him so we can stand before the Lord. God sees us through Jesus-colored glasses.

The love of God is reflected in the life of Jesus and how He came to set the captives free. All the gospels show a passionate God who restores health to the sick, rescues the demonized, revives the oppressed, redeems the sinners, recovers the outcasts, raises the dead, and renews our faith in God alone. Jesus never ran away from anyone. He ran to them. He came to represent the heart of the Father.

Speaking of love, look deeper at what love is, according to the Bible.

Love is large and incredibly patient. Love is gentle and consistently kind to all. It refuses to be jealous when blessing comes to someone else. Love does not brag about one's achievements nor inflate its own importance. Love does not traffic in shame and disrespect, nor selfishly seek its own honor. Love is not easily irritated or quick to take offense. Love joyfully celebrates honesty and finds no delight in what is wrong. Love is a safe place of shelter, for it never stops believing the best for others. Love never takes failure as defeat, for it never gives up. (1 Corinthians 13:4–7)

This is a reflection of Jesus. So many Scriptures back up that all He did was in love.

As we can see, love is very different than the world tries to show us. Movies show us if you fall out of love with your spouse, it's okay to leave, yet the Bible teaches us that love endures all things. Social media encourages pride and inflating your ego through video, posts, and memes. Therapists write off individuals as unlovable or incapable of changing. In this all-about-me culture, we fail to recognize it's actually all about love—it's all about Jesus.

The life of Jesus was not filled with the religiosity of the priests and Pharisees; no, He hung out with the misfits and outcasts. He went out spreading love and releasing many that were afflicted. Mary Magdala is one example; Jesus cast seven demons out of her, and now, she was His follower. That is what happens when love comes through and sets you free.

Since becoming a believer in Christ and following Him, I have seen what His love can do. The most powerful prayer I ever prayed completely revolutionized me. I didn't understand what I was asking at the time, but the Father was more than willing to grant my request with a great big yes. I prayed that He would give me His heart for people. You sometimes ask God for something, not realizing how it will radically change your life.

The Lord began showing me His love for His daughters that had been abused, rejected, discounted, and replaced. They shared the stories at church, work, coffee shops, grocery stores, the mall, restaurants, and pretty much wherever I traveled. My heart broke as each woman recounted her tale of heartbreak or trauma. God gave me such a love for women, because He told me, "You can't minister to those you don't love." Soon, He gave me a heart for those lost in false religions and new age and those with mental disorders.

I was at my friend Cathy's house for her daughter's graduation party. Her sister Ginny had come down the day before, and her daughter brought a friend with her. The minute I saw this young girl, her friend, I was surprised because I thought she was very unattractive and even ugly. This was not how I normally saw people or how I thought of them. The heart of the Father for people helped me see past the physical to their true beauty inside. The young lady in her late teens was extremely shy and distanced herself from me. We all hung out, laughing, chatting, and preparing for the party the next day. I was sharing some of my God stories, and Ginny listened intently. She got up and hugged me tightly as we said goodbye until the next day. Healing needed to take place, and God was preparing the atmosphere for it to happen.

The next day, we all gathered to celebrate KK's graduation. The party was in full swing when Ginny sat down beside me. She said, "You know that Marcie needs to talk to you."

I said, "Okay, what does she need?"

Ginny began unpacking all the trauma this young girl had gone through: in and out of mental hospitals and issues with her parents. She looked at me with tears in her eyes. "Can you do the God thing with her and help her?"

I told her, "Absolutely, I will. But you need to tell her what I do so she can make a choice." Ginny hugged me and ran off to find Marcie.

Within a few minutes, she returned with Marcie, both of them with a huge smile. I said, "So you would like to talk with me?"

Marcie nodded. I pulled her over to a quiet corner of the patio where we could talk privately. I sat down and looked her in the eyes and asked her if Ginny told her what I do. She said yes, she did. The Holy Spirit then told me that she thought I was a psychic. I smiled. "Do you think I'm a psychic?"

She said, "Aren't you?"

I told her, "No, I'm not, but I do hear from God, and I hear very well." She began twisting in the chair as I continued explaining. "I can help you. I pray through Jesus and with the Holy Spirit. If you allow me, we can get you free."

She replied, "I'm going back to church, so you can pray over me."

I asked if I could hold her hand, and she placed her hand in mine. The Holy Spirit started to show me movies that were all about witchcraft. I then saw a crystal amulet spinning above a mortar bowl. "Do you watch movies about witchcraft?"

She said, "Yes, I do." I then asked if she had any crystal amulets that she may have used. She told me, "Oh yeah, I've cast spells with them." My jaw dropped. Never doubt what the Holy Spirit shows you.

I would never have thought that this young lady was actually a practicing witch. I started sharing what the Holy Spirit was showing me, telling her that she watched those movies because she believed all the lies that the witchcraft spells would make her more popular and beautiful. God started to reveal His great love for this very lost and confused young lady. He began to speak to her brokenness, insecurity, fear, confusion, anger, rejection, and the abandonment she had felt since middle school. I shared the most intimate details with compassion and tenderness that only Jesus could supply.

After all that, Marcie was in tears as she understood that God really did know and see her. I looked at her again in the eyes. "If you are ready, we can get you free." Sobbing, she nodded in agreement. I told her to repent for any and all witchcraft, curses, and spells she had been involved in. To repent for being rebellious and disobedient and not honoring her parents. To repent for following other gods and believing their lies over God's truth. After she repented, I told her it was time to forgive those that hurt, lied, abused, rejected, abandoned, and traumatized her. She repeated willingly all the things the Holy Spirit was revealing to me. I then asked her if she would put her hand on her heart and if I could place mine on top of hers. She said yes, and I began to pray over her heart for healing of all the wounds.

I said, "Okay, are you ready to kick these demons to the curb?" Again, she nodded in confirmation and began renouncing all the things the Holy Spirit showed me. I then put my hand on her head and told all those spirits to leave quietly with no manifestations. The heaviness lifted as the spirits that she unknowingly gave access to departed. There was no battle because she broke all the rights they had over her, and so at the name of Jesus, they left.

Something was different in Marcie now. She was beautiful. It was like looking at a different person. I grabbed her hand and led her to the bathroom to see the new Marcie in the mirror. As soon as she caught her reflection, shock came over her as she could not believe her eyes. The tears highlighted her now crystal-blue eyes; her formerly white pasty skin was now full of color as her checks had a pink glow. We were both crying at this dramatic change. I said, "You haven't seen that face in a long time."

The tears streamed down her cheeks, confirming what I said. She replied, "A really long time."

Back at our seats on the patio, I asked if she wanted to give her life to Jesus. She did, so we prayed the sinner's prayer, and I asked the Holy Spirit to fill any places that were unoccupied so that nothing could return. After we finished, joy replaced the previous depression. We began giggling like a couple of schoolgirls as the Holy

Spirit was removing all traces of sadness and fear. The anxiety was gone, and so was insecurity as she began to open up to this new life. I shared the truth of how I saw her when I first met her. "I wasn't seeing you, sweetie, but I was seeing that ugly, oppressive spirit you were carrying. Now look at you. What a change! You were always beautiful, but that spirit was trying to hide you." She hugged and thanked me for the prayers. I told her that Papa loved her so much and that she needed to thank Jesus because He did all the work. I was simply His assistant.

The more I watch God minister, the more His love astounds me. I have witnessed Him reveal Himself to those that the church doesn't want. The Father once told me that He was through with religion because religion kept His children from Him. He said He was going to raise up a new church that would act and do as He says. I had no idea at the time that I would be a part of that church. Obedience is the key that opens the door of love to others.

People have commented on my obedience to all the Father tells me to do. I have argued with Him and tried to talk my way out of His instructions, but when it comes down to it, I do what He says. We don't understand why God does what He does, but we know God always has a plan. "For My thoughts are not your thoughts, Nor are your ways My ways," says the Lord" (Isaiah 55:8 NKJV). If God is love, then we shouldn't be afraid of what He is asking us to do because it's all done in love.

God has thanked me for caring for a lost son or feeding a homeless person. God has apologized when I have gone through hard lessons or been mistreated. He knows the desires of our hearts, and He shows us that He sees even the littlest details of our lives. He knew my heart longed to have a dog, but the timing just wasn't right. I began praying about adopting a dog and started to dream with God about it.

The vision was clear as I could see the black-and-white face of a border collie. I started to hint to Rob about the possibility of having a dog. This time, I didn't get the quick rejection and excuses as to why it was not the right time. We were moving to a new house with a huge fenced-in backyard. As I prayed, I asked the Lord to lead me to my dog. I went on the web, searching for border collie puppies near me. A litter had just arrived, forty-five minutes from our house. I called to inquire if the puppies were still available. Only one was left. He was named Mr. T, but someone was going to look at him the next day. I asked if I could see him that day. The sweet lady agreed.

I picked up the kids after school and rushed to see this pup. He had been pulled from the rest of the litter because he had mange. He was now healthy enough to be adopted. I pulled up to the school and told the kids, "I have a surprise for you." We drove to the animal shelter, and I told them about Mr. T, who might be our new puppy. We walked in and asked to see him. He was in a cage, frightened and anxious. The staff took him out and put us in a room together. He was rambunctious as soon as he was free. He licked the kids, and it was instant love. We decided to take Mr. T home with us that day. I filled out the adoption papers, bought a leash, and took him to the car. He was excited as the kids piled into the back seat. I had brought a blanket with me and laid it between the kids.

At home with our new puppy, we changed his name to Elvis. Rob was not happy at first, but he, too, couldn't help falling in love with the dog. We got a book on border collies and a cage to help potty train him. Elvis hated the cage and made a bigger mess when he was in it than when he was out. So we gated the kitchen instead, and soon, Elvis was house-trained. He was such a smart dog and understood so many commands. He had certain genetic traits that he exhibited around others. For example, he was a herding dog, so he was constantly herding not only my children but any child that visited our house. To Elvis, children were his sheep, and he was there to take care of them.

Elvis had another special trait: He could see in the spirit. When I prayed, Elvis looked around or lay beside me as the angels entered the room. We loved Elvis, and God knew it. I have heard that God loves what and who we love, and one day, He proved it.

One cold, rainy, damp fall day in New Jersey, soup was the dinner and pjs the attire. The kids were at school, so I was enjoying my coffee and scrolling through Facebook. The rain had stopped as I looked out my bay window. I had a blanket wrapped around me, and Elvis was lying next to me. I smiled and petted his sweet head. He licked me as I began laughing for him to stop. The Lord gently spoke to me. "Take Elvis to the park." I shook my head and wondered where that thought came from. I looked outside again; the rain had stopped. I got up to get some more coffee when the Lord repeated, "Take Elvis to the park."

I thought, *Wait a second. Why would I want to go to the park? It's gross outside.* I called Elvis and went to the back sliding glass door. I opened it up and told him to go outside. He looked at me with the saddest eyes and refused to go out.

Then God spoke a third time. He was telling me not to be selfish and to take my dog to the park to run. I put on my sneakers and jacket and picked up my umbrella in case it started to rain again. I looked at Elvis. "You want to go to the park?" He began jumping around as I found his leash, and we headed to the car.

At the dog park, a few people, maybe five or so, were there. It would be a short visit. We walked through the special gate that protected dogs from escaping. I took off his leash, and away he ran. I giggled as I watched him run and enjoy the freedom he so loved. He was interacting with the other dogs as he was friendly, but I kept an eye out to make sure that none of the dogs became aggressive. I apologized to God for being so lazy and thanked Him for making me come. I loved Elvis and loved to see him happy. I breathed in the cool, crisp air when something caught my attention: Elvis and another dog playing.

But this was more than just playing. I saw love like in dog movies where the two dogs fall in love. Elvis and this other dog were standing up on their hind legs with paws in the air like a hug. I never saw anything like it. I was watching something special.

A young woman came over and watched the dogs playing. I asked, "Excuse me, is that your dog?"

She said, "Yes, she is."

I said, "That's mine," pointing at Elvis. "Is your dog a border collie?"

The lady answered, "Yes, she is, and she is also part lab."

I got excited as I told her that Elvis was too. She told me that her dog was born in December and would soon be turning one. I told her that my dog was the same age. The lady turned and asked me where I got my dog. I told her the name of the animal shelter that was forty-five minutes away.

She asked, "Is that Mr. T?" I gasped, and my jaw dropped at the mention of his given shelter name.

"Yes, how did you know?"

"Because we almost adopted him. That's his sister he is playing with. We couldn't adopt him because he got mange, so we took his sister instead."

I was overcome with emotion. God wanted me to take Elvis to the dog park so that he could reconnect with his sister.

We were both in awe as the siblings ran and played together. I never saw such happiness in my dog, and I had almost missed it. I began thanking God for being persistent with me. Missy, who owned Elvis's sister, and I decided that we would plan to get together again. I asked if next time, I could bring the kids, and she said absolutely.

We got together a few more times and let the dogs play. The kids were so excited to meet his sister and watch them run. Our schedules grew complicated, so it became more difficult figuring out times to meet. We met one last time so they could say goodbye.

On that special day when Elvis reconnected with his sister, God reminded me that He is able to do exceedingly, abundantly, far above all we can ask, think, or imagine, according to Ephesians 3:20. He is the God of the universe, and He knows how to reach anyone. He put two strangers together in a dog park to show me that He cares about things I love.

My dog, Elvis, was such an important part of our lives. On December 16, 2020, as I held him, we had to say goodbye to our fur baby, which was the hardest thing I ever had to do. Elvis would be waiting for us in heaven, so this goodbye was only for now. Once he was gone, Jesus gave me a vision of Elvis licking His face in heaven. Dogs are in heaven; I've seen mine there. Our love is never wasted and is valued by God. He takes care of our fur babies till we can see them again.

Over the years, my relationship with the Father has continued to grow deeper and more secure. He gave me this book to write and told me the title. In a vision, He showed me what the cover would look like, and then He brought the right person to create it. I was encouraged through every step of this process, always knowing He was by my side. Nothing is too big to accomplish when you have the Father next to you. I've learned how to do hard things and have marveled as I successfully completed them all with God's help.

He has loved me back from brokenness and renewed my voice when I thought it was stolen. The Father has fought on my behalf and has vindicated me. Prayers have been answered within hours, and situations have turned around instantly. He carries my heart, and I carry His. We have more than a friendship; we have a true father-and-daughter relationship. Just when I think Papa can't love me more, He surprises me yet again.

In September 2022, I was preparing for my sixth annual Daddy's Girl Women's Conference on the Jersey shore. My friend texted me that she had purchased another room and registered her friend Greta who might come with her. The theme was "Meet Me at the Well," based on the story of the woman at the well in John 4.

People from all over the country had registered. They were flying in from the west coast and driving up the east coast. Some of my closest friends couldn't attend due to prior commitments. I understood, but I was still sad that I wouldn't see them. Since the pandemic, I hadn't seen some friends since right before the country shut down. I was trying to get to Margie Moorman's conference in Galveston, but no matter how I tried, I just couldn't make it happen. (I called her Momma Margie.)

I was excited about those who were attending and preparing for all the ladies. I picked up my crew and speakers the day before the conference. They were helping me pack up the goody bags and make the name tags. Amie commented on Greta's name tag. "Wow, that is an old-fashioned name. Who is Greta?" I told her that it was Audrey's friend who was coming, and she was really excited about it.

We had a family dinner at my house the night before we left for the shore. That's when I began missing my mommas. How I wished that Momma Margie and Momma Karen could be with me. In 2017, at my first conference, Margie was one of my speakers. That was where she became my spiritual momma. Since then, God has blessed me with two more spiritual mommas: Momma Karen and Momma Robin. All three of these ladies had ministered to me regarding my mother wounds and were the reason I was still in ministry.

Once at the event, we set up, and I went to my room to shower for the evening session. As I was getting ready, Papa told me that the relationships that He put in my life would flourish and grow. He said, "I have surprises for you, and you will see who is for you." I smiled and thanked Him for all His goodness.

My friend Ryan is more than my producer; he's a spiritual son. He texted me that he needed me to take pictures. He wanted all the speakers gathered together for a group shot. Not everyone was there yet, so I was leaving to pick them up. Ryan stopped me. "I need you to stay so I can take pictures." I told him I would be back soon, as I just needed to pick up Robin. He said, "No, Lisa, you are going to block your blessing."

I thought, *Well, he must have something he is putting together, so I need to let him take his pictures.*

As he was taking my picture, he said, "Someone wants to say hi." I turned, and there was Momma Margie walking toward me. My knees buckled, and the tears streamed down my face.

I asked, "When did you get here?" She said she had arrived the night before and a mutual friend had picked her up. I asked, "Why didn't you tell me you were coming?"

Two weeks earlier, Papa had told her that He wanted her to go to New Jersey and surprise me. The tears started again as God had told me just a few hours earlier that He had a surprise for me. He wanted to do something special for me. He knew I wanted to see Momma Margie but couldn't make it work. So He came up with a plan so I could see my momma, and He orchestrated it all.

I told Momma Margie, "You need to stay here with us." She told me she was. I replied, "You did? I didn't see your name!"

Right then, she grabbed me, looked me in the eyes, and shouted, "I'm *Greta*!"

In the last scene in the movie *Ghost* with the late actor Patrick Swayze, he says to his wife as he is leaving earth and encountering heaven, "It's amazing, Molly. The love inside, you take it with you."[1] I believe that is the truth. When I minister, the one constant I can always feel is the love of the Father. His love has changed me and is still changing me. With each encounter, I see a new perspective of His love for His children. I have more fun going on adventures with the Father than I can begin to say. He has blessed me so that I have met and connected with people when it seemed impossible; then again, He is the God of the impossible. I have learned He can get to anyone at any time and make anything happen. His love has given me wings to move to higher places and allows me to see with a heavenly perspective.

The Father has opened doors for me to walk through and given me a platform to share with others. My talk shows, *Touched by Prayer* and *Crown Chats*, give me so many opportunities to share His love. I know who I am because I know that I am loved, and that has made all the difference in my prayers.

And He wants to do the same for you. Will you let Him?

Love:

Heavenly Father, I thank you for your love. Lord, you showed us this love on Calvary, this love that was poured out by your Son, Jesus Christ, for me, this love that was poured out for the world. Lord, I thank you that the Word says that your perfect love casts out all fears. Fill me with that perfect love so that any doubt or any fear leaves instantly. Help me keep love as my focus. Let love be my language. Let love be my purpose. Help me speak with patience, with kindness. Keep me from jealousy and pride. Let my words speak honor and joy. Hold back my anger and help me walk in compassion. Father, make me a safe place for others. Let me love what you love and love who you love. Allow me to be a part of the love revolution that you have assembled here on earth. I ask you to let others see your love inside me. Fill me to overflowing with your love, in Jesus's name. Amen.

Notes

FOREWORD

1. Dick Eastman, *No Easy Road: Discover the Extraordinary Power of Personal Prayer,* (Ada, Michigan: Baker Publishing Group, 2003) N/A.

2. OBEDIENCE

1. "75 Mighty Bible Scriptures on Obedience," Connect Us, October 20, 2019, https://connectusfund.org/75-mighty-bible-scriptures-on-obedience.
2. Chris Poblete, "The Names of God: Jehovah-Raah," The BLB Blog, July 25, 2012 https://blogs.blueletterbible.org/blb/2012/07/25/the-names-of-god-jehovah-raah/.

3. PERSONAL AND SPIRITUAL RELATIONSHIP

1. Colossians 2:5 says, "For though I am absent in the flesh, yet I am with you in spirit, rejoicing to see your good order and the steadfastness of your faith in Christ" (NKJV). Paul is referring to his presence with the Colossians, whether physically or in the spirit. In the same way, at times, we can be present with others in the spirit as well.

4. FAITH AND TRUST

1. *Merriam-Webster*, s.v. "trust (*n.*)," accessed December 6, 2022, https://www.merriam-webster.com/dictionary/trust.
2. *Merriam-Webster*, s.v. "faith (*n.*)," accessed December 6, 2022, https://www.merriam-webster.com/dictionary/faith.
3. For more information on an orphan mentality, see the resources at www.shiloh place.org, especially this handout https://www.shilohplace.org/orphan-son-handout.

6. NAMES OF GOD AND COVENANT

1. Encyclopedia Britannica Online, s.v. "Abraham," accessed December 6, 2022, https://www.britannica.com/biography/Abraham.
2. John Paul Jackson, *I AM: 365 Names of God* (North Sutton, New Hampshire, Streams Publications, 2002).
3. Brian Simmons, *The Passion Translation*, "Introduction to Hebrews," YouVersion, accessed December 6, 2022, https://www.bible.com/bible/1849/HEB. INTRO1.TPT.
4. Charles John Ellicott, *Ellicott's Commentary for English Readers*, "Genesis 16," Bible Hub, accessed December 6, 2022, https://biblehub.com/commentaries/ellicott/genesis/16.htm.

8. WORSHIP AND PRAISE

1. *Merriam-Webster*, s.v. "worship (*n*.)," accessed December 6, 2022, https://www.merriam-webster.com/dictionary/worship.
2. *King James Bible Dictionary*, s.v. "honor (*n*.)," accessed December 6, 2022, https://kingjamesbibledictionary.com/Dictionary/honour.
3. *Merriam-Webster*, s.v. "reverence (*n*.)," accessed December 6, 2022, https://www.merriam-webster.com/dictionary/reverence.
4. *Merriam-Webster*, s.v. "devotion (*n*.)," accessed December 6, 2022, https://www.merriam-webster.com/dictionary/devotion.
5. *Jewish English Lexicon*, s.v. "Tehillim (*n*.)," accessed December 6, 2022, https://jel.jewish-languages.org/words/2289.
6. These words referred to the following verse. "Your eyes saw my substance, being yet unformed. And in Your book they all were written, the days fashioned for me, when as yet there were none of them" (Psalms 139:16 NKJV). God has a book in heaven about each of us.
7. See Isaiah 53.

9. PRAYING IN TONGUES AND SEEING IN THE SPIRIT

1. "Lexicon :: Strong's G1100 – glossa," Blue Letter Bible, accessed December 6, 2022, https://www.blueletterbible.org/lexicon/g1100/kjv/tr/0-1/.

10. REPENTANCE AND FORGIVENESS

1. "Lexicon :: Strong's G3340 – metanoeō," Blue Letter Bible, accessed December 6, 2022, https://www.blueletterbible.org/lexicon/g3340/kjv/tr/0-1/.
2. *Merriam-Webster*, s.v. "pride (*n*.)," accessed December 6, 2022, https://www.

merriam-webster.com/dictionary/pride.
3. "Resentment is Like Taking Poison and Waiting for the Other Person to Die," Quote Investigator, accessed December 6, 2022, https://quoteinvestigator. com/2017/08/19/resentment/.

12. LOVE

1. "*Ghost*, Patrick Swayze: Sam Wheat," IMDB, accessed December 6, 2022, https://www.imdb.com/title/tt0099653/characters/nm0000664.

About the Author

Lisa Perna began a life-changing journey with God in November 2009 when she encountered the Holy Spirit. She has developed a deeper relationship with God and now walks in signs, wonders, and miracles, leading others into personal encounters with the living God.

Since 2014, Lisa has hosted a weekly talk show, *Touched by Prayer*, and a daily morning prophetic devotional broadcast, *Crown Chats*. In 2017, God prompted her to hold Daddy's Girl Women's Conferences so that others could learn their identity as sons and daughters.

Lisa is married to Rob, the man behind the scenes for the last 27 years. She has two beautiful children, Alexander and Samantha, and her constant companion is Cash, a six-year-old rescue Australian Cattle Dog.

facebook.com/tbptalkshow

twitter.com/touchedbyprayer

instagram.com/touchedbyprayer

youtube.com/@touchedbyprayertv7425